BUSY BEES
FALL

Fun for Two's and Three's

By Elizabeth McKinnon and Gayle Bittinger

Illustrated by Barb Tourtillotte

Warren Publishing House, Inc., Everett, Washington

We wish to thank the following teachers, childcare workers, and parents for contributing some of the ideas in this book: Betty Ruth Baker, Waco, TX; Deborah Balmer, Mesa, AZ; Lynn Beaird, Loma Linda, CA; Ellen Bedford, Bridgeport, CT; Lori Gross Bergy, Harrisonburg, VA; Janice Bodenstedt, Jackson, MI; Sue Brown, Louisville, KY; Susan Burbridge, Albuquerque, NM; Patricia Coyne, Mansfield, MA; Marjorie Debowy, Stony Brook, NY; Irmgard Fuertges, Kitchener, Ontario; Rita J. Galloway, Harlingen, TX; Rosemary Giordano, Philadelphia, PA; Kathy Gonion, Elk Grove Village, IL; Barbara Hasson, Portland, OR; Nancy Heimark, Alamogordo, NM; Janet Helgaas, Luverne, MN; Dee Hoffman, Aitkin, MN; Julie Israel, Ypsilanti, MI; Barbara H. Jackson, Denton, TX; Ellen Javernick, Loveland, CO; Karen Kilimnik, Philadelphia, PA; Martha T. Lyon, Fort Wayne, IN; Kathy McCullough, Everett, WA; Susan A. Miller, Kutztown, PA; Donna Mullennix, Thousand Oaks, CA; Diana Nazaruk, Clark Lake, MI; Judy Panko, Aitkin, MN; Susan M. Paprocki, Northbrook, IL; Barbara Paxson, Warren, OH; Susan Peters, Upland, CA; Jeanne Petty, Camden, DE; Lois E. Putnam, Pilot Mountain, NC; Beverly Qualheim, Marquette, MI; Polly Reedy, Elmhurst, IL; Vicki Reynolds, East Hanover, NJ; Deborah A. Roessel, Flemington, NJ; Vicki Shannon, Napton, MO; Betty Silkunas, Lansdale, PA; Diane Thom, Maple Valley, WA; Margaret Timmons, Fairfield, CT; Elizabeth Vollrath, Stevens Point, WI; Bobbie Lee Wagman, Milton, WI; Gail Weidner, Tustin, CA; Maryann Zucker, Reno, NV; Deborah Zumbar, Alliance, OH.

Editorial Staff:

Editorial Manager: Kathleen Cubley
Editors: Susan Hodges, Jean Warren
Copy Editor: Kris Fulsaas
Proofreader: Mae Rhodes
Editorial Assistant: Erica West

Design and Production Staff:

Art Manager: Jill Lustig
Book Design: Lynne Faulk
Layout Production: Sarah Ness
Cover Design: Brenda Mann Harrison
Digital Coloring: Kathy Kotomaimoce
Cover Illustration: Barb Tourtillotte
Busy Bee Drawings: Susan Dahlman
Production Manager: Jo Anna Brock

ISBN 1-57029-008-3

Library of Congress Catalog Number 93-61897
Printed in the United States of America
Published by: Warren Publishing House, Inc.
          P.O. Box 2250
          Everett, WA 98203

20 19 18 17 16 15 14 13 12 11 10 9 8 7 6 5 4 3 2 1

INTRODUCTION

Welcome to the Fall edition of *Busy Bees—Fun for Two's and Three's,* an idea resource for teachers and parents of children 2 to 3 years old.

Busy Bees—Fun for Two's and Three's offers age-appropriate, fun, attention-getting activities. It is filled with hands-on projects and movement games that are just right for busy little ones. Also included are language and snack suggestions suitable for two's and three's, plus a rhyme and one or more songs to accompany each chapter.

The ideas in this book are designed to complement your everyday curriculum. The chapters are listed in an order that you may wish to follow day by day, although each one stands alone and can be used in a pick-and-choose fashion. You will find that the activities are perfect for those times when you want to interject group participation and purposefulness into your usual free-play agenda.

We hope that the suggestions in *Busy Bees—Fun for Two's and Three's* will act as a catalyst and inspire you to add ideas and activities of your own to those in the book.

Happy teaching!

CONTENTS

November

SEPTEMBER

Apples

Picking Up Apples

Place a basket on the floor. Let your children take turns picking up pretend apples and putting them into the basket while everyone sings the following song.

Sung to: "The Paw-Paw Patch"

Pick up the apples, put 'em in the basket,
Pick up the apples, put 'em in the basket,
Pick up the apples, put 'em in the basket,
Way down yonder by the apple tree.

Jean Warren

RHYME

Look at the Apple

Look at the apple I have found,
   (Form circle with hands.)
So round and rosy on the ground.
Mother will wash it and cut it in two,
   (Pretend to wash and cut apple.)
Half for me and half for you.
   (Hold out one palm, then the other.)

Martha T. Lyon

HANDS-ON LEARNING GAME

Apple Colors

Set out a basket of red and green apples and pieces of red and green construction paper. Let your children remove the apples from the basket and place them on the matching colored paper pieces. When the children are ready for a more challenging game, add some yellow apples and a piece of yellow construction paper.

I'm a Little Apple

Sung to: "I'm a Little Teapot"

I'm a little apple,
Short and round.
I make a crunchy,
Munchy sound.
If you bite into me,
You will see
I'm delicious as can be!

Barbara Paxson

Munching Apples

Sung to: "If You're Happy and You Know It"

If you like to munch apples,
Raise your hand.
If you like to munch apples,
Raise your hand.
If you like to hear them crunch,
And eat them for your lunch,
If you like to munch apples,
Raise your hand.

Repeat, each time substituting a different
action for *raise your hand.*

Jean Warren

LANGUAGE IDEA

Make up a story about what is
inside an apple. At the end of the
story, cut open an apple to reveal
the seeds.

SNACK IDEA

Serve several different kinds of
apple slices for your children to
taste and compare.

Apple Trees

Apple Picking

Cut a tree shape out of felt and place it on a flannelboard. Cut out several felt apple shapes and put them into a basket. Let your children help place the apple shapes on the tree shape. Then let them take turns picking the apples from the tree as everyone counts together.

Variation: Ask older children to pick specific colors or sizes of apples.

MOVEMENT

Apple Ladder

Place a set of steps against a cupboard to represent a ladder leaning against an apple tree. Help each child in turn climb the steps and "pick" an apple that you have placed on top of the cupboard. Then help the child climb down the steps and put the apple into a basket on the floor.

RHYME

Two Green Apples

Way up high
In an apple tree,
  (Raise arms high.)
Two green apples
Smiled at me.
  (Smile.)

So I shook that tree
As hard as I could,
  (Pretend to shake tree.)
And down fell the apples.
Mmmm, they were good!
  (Rub tummy.)

Repeat, substituting *red*, then *yellow*, for *green*.

Adapted Traditional

Four Red Apples

Sung to: "This Old Man"

Four red apples in the tree,
Two for you and two for me.
So, shake that tree and watch them fall.
One, two, three, four—that is all.

Additional verses: Four green apples in the tree; Four yellow apples in the tree.

Jean Warren

LANGUAGE IDEA

Use the flannelboard shapes from the activity Apple Picking (page 10) to tell a story about an apple in an apple tree.

SNACK IDEA

Serve apple juice or apple cider.

Applesauce

Making Applesauce

3 to 4 sweet apples
½ cup water
½ teaspoon cinnamon

Let your children help wash and dry the apples. After you peel, core, and quarter the apples, have the children use table knives to cut the quarters in half. Place the apple pieces in a saucepan and let the children add the water and cinnamon. Simmer, covered, until the apples are tender, about 20 minutes. When the mixture has cooled, let the children mash the apples with a potato masher. Makes 6 small servings.

MOVEMENT

Apple Mash

Let your children pretend to pick up apples from the ground and toss them into a big cooking pot. Then play lively music and have them stomp around, pretending to mash the apples with their feet.

RHYME

If You Want Applesauce

I'm a little apple,
Growing on a tree.
If you want applesauce,
Just mash me!

Polly Reedy

SONG

Applesauce

Sung to: "Yankee Doodle"

Peel an apple,
Cut it up,
Cook it in a pot.
When you taste it,
You will find
It's applesauce you've got!

Martha T. Lyon

LANGUAGE IDEA

Make a set of picture cards showing how apples are made into applesauce. After doing the activity Making Applesauce (page 12), use the cards to talk about the activity with your children.

SNACK IDEA

Let your children enjoy their homemade applesauce from the activity Making Applesauce (page 12). Give them slices of raw apple to taste and compare with the applesauce.

Peanut Butter

Peanut Butter Playdough

¾ cup peanut butter
¾ cup toasted wheat germ
¼ cup honey
¼ cup powdered milk

Place all the ingredients in a small bowl and mix well. Divide the playdough into six pieces and give them to your children to play with. Because this play-dough is edible, make sure that the playing surface and utensils the children use have been thoroughly cleaned.

MOVEMENT

Peanut Butter Slide

With your children, pretend to grind up peanuts to make peanut butter. Then let the children slide back and forth across the floor, pretending to spread their peanut butter over giant pieces of bread.

RHYME

Peanut, Peanut Butter

Peanut, peanut butter,
(Pound fists together.)
Jelly!
(Open hands and hold them up.)
Peanut, peanut butter,
(Pound fists together.)
Jelly!
(Open hands and hold them up.)

First you dig 'em,
(Pretend to dig.)
You dig 'em, you dig 'em,
Dig 'em, dig 'em.

Additional verses: Then you crack 'em (*Open and close fists.*); Then you spread 'em (*Make spreading motions with two fingers of one hand.*); Then you eat 'em (*Pretend to eat sandwich.*). Repeat first verse at end of rhyme.

Author Unknown

Peanut Butter

Sung to: "Frere Jacques"

Peanut butter, peanut butter,
Good for you, fun to chew.
Spread it on a sandwich,
Spread it on a cracker.
Good for you, fun to chew.

Susan Peters

Peanut Butter Tracks

Sung to: "Down by the Station"

Down by the station
Early in the morning,
See the little peanuts
Sitting on the tracks.
See the little train
Chugging 'cross those peanuts.
Oh, oh, look out—
Peanut butter tracks!

Jean Warren

LANGUAGE IDEA

Ask your children to name different foods they like to eat with peanut butter.

SNACK IDEA

Serve peanut butter on crackers, bread, or apple slices.

Tastes

Paper-Plate Foods

Give each of your children a small paper plate. Set out a variety of food stickers. Let the children choose four or five stickers each and attach them to their paper plates. When they have finished, encourage the children to tell you how the different sticker foods taste.

MOVEMENT

Sweet and Sour

Have your children stand in an open area. Let them start hopping around as you name sweet foods. Whenever they hear you say "Sour pickle!" have them drop to the floor. Continue the game as long as interest lasts.

RHYME

Tastes

A kitten likes to taste tuna,
A mouse likes to taste cheese.
Katie likes to taste strawberries,
So pass the strawberries, please!

(Pretend to pass food and taste it.)

Repeat, each time substituting the name of one of your children for *Katie* and the name of a favorite food for *strawberries*.

Elizabeth McKinnon

LANGUAGE IDEA

Give each of your children a cube of cheese speared on a pretzel stick. Have the children eat their cheese cubes, then their pretzels, and tell how each food tastes and feels in their mouths.

SNACK IDEA

Serve a sweet-sour snack, such as lemonade garnished with lemon slices.

SONG

Taste Your Snack

Sung to: "I'm a Little Teapot"

It is time for us
To have our snack.
Please sit down
With hands in your lap.
Wait until everyone
Is served some food.
Then taste your snack,
Yum, yum, it's good!

Patricia Coyne

Fall Leaves

RHYME

Leaves, Leaves

Leaves, leaves,
Falling down,
Falling on the ground.
Red and yellow,
Orange and brown,
Leaves are falling down.

Susan A. Miller

HANDS-ON ART

Dried Leaf Art

Give each of your children a large leaf shape cut from yellow construction paper. Set out bowls of dried autumn leaves. Let the children brush glue on their leaf shapes. Then have them crumble the dried leaves and sprinkle the pieces all over the glue.

MOVEMENT

Falling Leaves

Ask your children to imagine that they are autumn leaves hanging on a tree and that you are the wind. Walk among the children and pretend to blow the leaves off the tree. Encourage the children to twirl and swirl as they slowly fall to the ground.

Leaves Are Twirling

Sung to: "Frere Jacques"

Leaves are twirling,
Leaves are twirling,
All around, all around.
They are falling softly,
Very, very softly,
To the ground, to the ground.

Barbara Paxson

LANGUAGE IDEA

As you recite the rhyme "Leaves, Leaves" (page 18), let your children make a pile of red, yellow, orange, and brown paper leaf shapes on the floor.

SNACK IDEA

Use a cookie cutter to cut leaf shapes out of buttered toast. Sprinkle on cinnamon sugar or top with fruit spreads in autumn colors.

Fall Trees

Counting Tree Leaves

Use a felt-tip marker to color a long, white glove brown. Cut small leaf shapes out of felt in autumn colors. Attach loops of tape rolled sticky side out to the backs of the shapes. Slip on the glove to turn your arm and hand into a "tree" and let your children attach the leaves to the finger "branches." Each time you remove the leaves, count them with the group.

MOVEMENT

Ring Around the Leaves

Take your children outside and have them make a big pile of leaves. Then let them hold hands and walk around their leaf pile as you sing the song below. When you sing the third line, have the children stop and toss handfuls of leaves up into the air.

Sung to: "Ring Around the Rosie"

Ring around the fall leaves,
Lots and lots of fall leaves.
Leaves. . . leaves. . .
They all fall down!

Lois E. Putnam

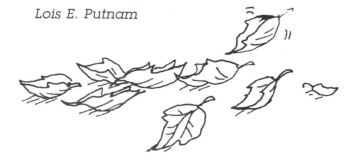

RHYME

Down by the Oak Tree

Down by the oak tree
On an autumn morning,
See all the yellow leaves
Whirling to and fro.
See how they twist and turn,
Whirling, whirling, whirling.
Down, down, down, down,
Away they blow.

As you recite the rhyme, have your children pretend to be leaves and act out the movements described.

Lois E. Putnam

SONG

The Leaves on the Trees

Sung to: "The Wheels on the Bus"

The leaves on the trees
Turn orange and red,
Orange and red,
Orange and red.
The leaves on the trees
Turn orange and red,
All through the town.

The leaves on the trees
Come twirling down,
Twirling down,
Twirling down.
The leaves on the trees
Come twirling down,
All through the town.

The leaves on the ground
Go swish, swish, swish,
Swish, swish, swish,
Swish, swish, swish.
The leaves on the ground
Go swish, swish, swish,
All through the town.

Irmgard Fuertges

LANGUAGE IDEA

Anchor a branch in a pot of soil
for a tree. Make up a fall story. As
you tell it, hang paper cutouts of
the characters on the tree.

SNACK IDEA

Serve a snack outside under an
autumn tree.

Friends

Find a Friend

For each pair of children, cut a different pair of matching shapes (circles, squares, stars, etc.) out of one color of construction paper. Mix up the shapes and give one to each child. Then have the children walk around and find their special friends by matching up their shapes.

Variation: Let your children match different pairs of colors instead of shapes.

Hint: Take part in the game yourself if you have an uneven number of children.

MOVEMENT

Hugs for Friends

Recite the rhyme "Love Your Friends" (this page). As you do so, let your children walk around giving hugs to you and to one another.

RHYME

Love Your Friends

Love your friends,
Love your friends,
Love them all the time.
Show them that
You care for them
By being good and kind.

Lori Gross Bergy

Won't You Be a Friend of Mine?

Sung to: "The Muffin Man"

Oh, won't you be a friend of mine,
A friend of mine, a friend of mine,
Oh, won't you be a friend of mine
And play with me today?

Yes, I'll be a friend of yours,
A friend of yours, a friend of yours,
Yes, I'll be a friend of yours
And play with you today.

Julie Israel

LANGUAGE IDEA

Give puppets to your children. Let them "make friends" by talking to one another through their puppets.

SNACK IDEA

Place two each of different snack items on your children's plates so that they can share with friends.

Getting Dressed

Paper Doll Fun

Purchase a set of paper dolls. Cut out the dolls, cover them with clear self-stick paper, and glue them, several inches apart, to an old non-aluminum baking sheet. Cut out the doll clothes, snip off the tabs, and cover the clothes with clear self-stick paper. Attach pieces of magnetic strip to the backs of the clothes. Let your children dress the paper dolls by placing the clothes on top of the dolls on the baking sheet. The magnetic strip pieces will keep the clothes in place until the children are ready to change the dolls' clothes.

MOVEMENT

Dressing Play

Let your children act out putting on different items of clothing such as shirts, pants, shoes, and socks. Then have them show how they put on hats, coats, boots, and mittens as you recite the rhyme "I Can Do It Myself" (this page).

RHYME

I Can Do It Myself

Hat on head, just like this,
  (Do actions as rhyme indicates.)
Pull it down, you see.
I can put my hat on
All by myself, just me.

One arm in, two arms in,
Buttons, one, two, three.
I can put my coat on
All by myself, just me.

Toes in first, heels push down,
Pull and pull, then see—
I can put my boots on
All by myself, just me.

Fingers here, thumbs right here,
Hands as warm as can be.
I can put my mittens on
All by myself, just me.

Adapted Traditional

LANGUAGE IDEA

Using a stuffed toy and doll clothes, tell a story about an animal that puts its clothes on all wrong when it gets dressed.

SNACK IDEA

Have your children wear improvised or pretend aprons for helping out at snacktime.

SONG

Getting Dressed

Sung to: "The Mulberry Bush"

This is the way we pull on our shirts,
Pull on our shirts, pull on our shirts.
This is the way we pull on our shirts,
So early in the morning.

This is the way we pull up our pants,
Pull up our pants, pull up our pants.
This is the way we pull up our pants,
So early in the morning.

Additional verses: This is the way we pull on our socks; This is the way we buckle our shoes; This is the way we put on our hats; This is the way we put on our coats; This is the way we pull on our boots; This is the way we put on our mittens.

Betty Silkunas

Socks

Sorting Socks

In a laundry basket, place pairs of different sizes and kinds of socks (baby socks, children's ankle and knee socks, men's and women's socks, athletic socks, nylon knee-highs, etc.). Mix up the socks well. Then let your children sort through the socks to find the matching pairs.

MOVEMENT

Sock Toss

Roll socks into balls and set out a large box. Give several sock balls to each child. Let your children stand back from the box and try tossing their sock balls into it while you sing the following song.

Sung to: "The Farmer in the Dell"

It's fun to toss the socks,
It's fun to toss the socks.
We toss the socks into the box,
It's fun to toss the socks.

Gayle Bittinger

RHYME

Stockings On

Deedle, deedle, dumpling,
   (Walk in stocking feet.)
Shoes all gone.
We went to town
With our stockings on.
Shoes all gone,
Stockings on.
Deedle, deedle, dumpling,
Shoes all gone.

Adapted Traditional

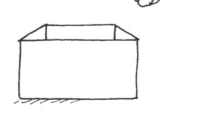

Marching in Our Socks

*Sung to: "When Johnny Comes
Marching Home"*

We're marching
In our socks today,
Hurray, hurray.
We've worked so hard
And now it's time
To play, to play.
We'll grab a hand
And march around.
Our stocking feet
Won't make a sound.
Oh, we're marching
In our socks
Today—hurray!

Jean Warren

Quiet Feet

Sung to: "The Farmer in the Dell"

Let's put on our socks,
Our super quiet socks.
We'll walk around without a sound
When we put on our socks.

As you sing, let your children walk, slide,
and tiptoe around in their stocking feet.

Jean Warren

Hide a familiar object, such as a
block or a spoon, inside a sock.
Tell a story about the object and
let your children try guessing
what the object is.

Use a Christmas cookie cutter to
make stocking-shaped cookies.
Let your children decorate the
cookies before eating them.

Squares

HANDS-ON ART
Square Collages
Cut squares of various sizes out of colored construction paper, wallpaper, and gift wrap. Give each of your children a large square of white construction paper. Let your children brush glue all over their large squares. Then have them arrange the colored squares on top of the glue to make collages.

MOVEMENT
Square Hop
Arrange carpet squares in a pathway on top of a large rug or other non-slick surface. Play music and let your children hop along the pathway from one carpet square to the next. When they reach the end of the path, have the children go back to the beginning and start their Square Hop again.

Variation: Instead of using carpet squares, tape squares of construction paper or posterboard to the floor.

RHYME
A Square Is Its Name
Here's a shape that you should know,
(Form square with fingers.)
A square is its name.
It has four corners and four sides
That measure all the same.

Author Unknown

SONGS

The Square Song
Sung to: "You Are My Sunshine"

I am a square, a lovely square.
I have four sides—they're all the same.
I have four corners, four lovely corners.
I am a square, that is my name.

Rita J. Galloway

It's a Square
Sung to: "Frere Jacques"

Here's a square, here's a square.
How can you tell? How can you tell?
It has four sides
All the same length.
It's a square, it's a square.

Jeanne Petty

LANGUAGE IDEA

Make a puppet by drawing a face on a 3-inch construction-paper square and attaching it to a craft stick. Let your children use the square puppet to tell stories they make up.

SNACK IDEA

Serve foods such as square crackers with matching cheese slices or square waffles.

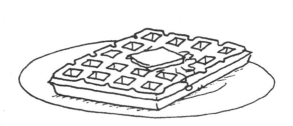

Boxes

A Little Box

A little box,
> *(Hold hands slightly apart.)*

A bigger box,
> *(Hold hands farther apart.)*

A great big box I see.
> *(Hold hands as far apart as possible.)*

Now let's count them.

Are you ready?

One,
> *(Hold hands as far apart as possible.)*

Two,
> *(Hold hands closer together.)*

Three.
> *(Hold hands slightly apart.)*

Adapted Traditional

HANDS-ON LEARNING GAME

Nesting Boxes

Collect several open boxes that will fit one inside the other. Nest the boxes and give them to one of your children. Let the child take the boxes apart and try nesting them again.

MOVEMENT

Box Play

Set out several cardboard cartons. Play music and let your children dance around the cartons, then inside them. Also, tape together large cartons, with ends removed, to make a tunnel for the children to crawl through.

A Great Big Box

Sung to: "I'm a Little Teapot"

There's a great big box
Down on the floor.
Someone cut out
A great big door.
Then they made a window
On the side,
So I can see
Who's playing inside.

There's a great big box
Down on the floor.
I like to open
And shut the door.
I like to go inside
And look around,
Then stick my head
Out the window I found.

Jean Warren

Boxes Everywhere

Sung to: "Twinkle, Twinkle, Little Star"

Boxes, boxes, everywhere,
Some are long, some are square.
Some I stack, when they are small,
Some so big, inside I crawl.
Boxes, boxes, everywhere,
Some are long, some are square.

Author Unknown

LANGUAGE IDEA

Hide a familiar object inside a small box. Let your children shake the box and try to guess what is inside as you give clues.

SNACK IDEA

For each of your children, prepare a "box lunch" by packing a snack, a paper napkin, and a plastic eating utensil in a box.

Jack-In-The-Boxes

Boxes for Jack

Give each of your children a cardboard carton that has been opened at the top. Have your children decorate the insides and outsides of their boxes with crayons. When they have finished, let them climb inside their decorated cartons and pretend to be jack-in-the boxes.

MOVEMENT

Jack, Jack

Read the rhyme below to your children. Have them crouch down near the floor at the beginning of the rhyme and jump up when you say, "Up you pop!"

Jack, Jack, down you go,
Down in your box, down so low.
Jack, Jack, there goes the top,
Quickly now, up you pop!

Author Unknown

RHYME

Jack-In-The-Box

Jack-in-the-box,
You sit so still.
  (Make fist with thumb inside.)
Won't you come out?
Yes, I will!
  (Pop out thumb.)

Adapted Traditional

Wake Up, Jack-In-The-Box

Sung to: "Twinkle, Twinkle, Little Star"

Wake up, wake up, jack-in-the-box,
Wake up, wake up, somebody knocks.
One time, two times, three times, four,
Jack pops out of his little square door.
Wake up, wake up, jack-in-the-box,
Wake up, wake up, somebody knocks.

Adapted Traditional

LANGUAGE IDEA

Hide your thumb inside your fist to represent a jack-in-the-box and tell a story about the toy. Pop up your thumb at the end of the story.

SNACK IDEA

Serve each of your children a "snack-in-the-box" such as a tiny box of raisins or a box of juice.

In and Out

HANDS-ON LEARNING GAME

In and Out the Tunnel

Select a long, wide cardboard tube and the largest toy car that will easily fit inside it. Prop up the tube. Let your children take turns putting the toy car in the top end of the tube and have everyone watch as it comes out the bottom end.

RHYME

In and Out

In and out, in and out,
In and out I go.
In and out, in and out,
Walking fast, then slow.

Repeat, substituting *hopping, running,* or *crawling* for *walking.*

Jean Warren

MOVEMENT

The Hokey-Pokey

Stand in a circle with your children. Then sing the song below and act out the movements together.

Sung to: "Hokey-Pokey"

You put your one foot in,
You put your one foot out,
You put your one foot in
And you shake it all about.
You do the hokey-pokey
And you turn yourself around.
That's what it's all about.

Additional verses: You put your two feet in; You put your one hand in; You put your two hands in; You put your little head in; You put your whole self in.

Adapted Traditional

SONG

Go In and Out the Circle

Sung to: "Go In and Out the Window"

Go in and out the circle,
Go in and out the circle.
Go in and out the circle,
As we have done before.

Stand with your children in a circle and hold hands. As you sing the song, step forward on *in* and backward on *out*.

Adapted Traditional

LANGUAGE IDEA

Use a dollhouse and toy figures to tell a story about going in and out of rooms, doors, the bathtub, etc.

SNACK IDEA

Have your children place snack foods in small paper cups and then take the foods out for eating.

Keys

HANDS-ON LEARNING GAME

Color Keys

Select several different-colored keys (available at locksmith shops). Arrange the keys on a square of posterboard and trace around each one to make a game board. Color each key shape to match the color of the traced key. Cover the game board with clear self-stick paper for durability. To play, have your children place the keys on top of the matching colored key shapes on the game board.

MOVEMENT

Locking and Unlocking

Give each of your children a small key chain with one or two keys on it. Let the children walk around the room pretending to lock and unlock doors, cabinets, trunks, etc., with their keys.

RHYME

Knock, Knock

Knock, knock,
   (Make knocking motions.)
Peek in.
   (Cup hand above eye.)
Unlock the door,
   (Pretend to turn key.)
And walk right in.
   (Open pretend door and step forward.)

Adapted Traditional

SONG

Helping Daddy Drive

Sung to: "Twinkle, Twinkle, Little Star"

Unlock the car door, climb inside,
I get to help my daddy drive.
Fasten my seat belt, put in the key,
Start the engine, one, two, three.
Turn the corner, step on the gas,
The road is clear, so we can pass.

Repeat, substituting *mommy* for *daddy*.

Adapted Traditional

LANGUAGE IDEA

Use a small suitcase with a key to tell a story about going on a trip. Lock and unlock the suitcase as part of the story.

SNACK IDEA

Make paper key shapes to match different-colored paper placemats. Let each of your children find a place at the snack table by matching a key to a placemat "door."

Spiders

Little Spider

See the little spider
Climbing up the wall.
> *(Crawl fingers up opposite arm.)*

See the little spider
Stumble and fall.
> *(Drop fingers quickly down arm.)*

See the little spider
Tumble down the street.
> *(Jump fingers down leg.)*

See the little spider
Stop down at my feet.
> *(Rest fingers on foot.)*

Author Unknown

HANDS-ON ART

Thumbprint Spiders

Make a paint pad by placing folded paper towels in a shallow container and pouring on a small amount of black tempera paint. Help each of your children in turn press a thumb on the paint pad, then on a piece of construction paper, to make prints. When the paint has dried, turn each thumbprint into a spider by using a fine-tip black marker to add eight legs.

Variation: Instead of making a paint pad, use a commercial stamp pad with washable black ink.

MOVEMENT

Spider Dance

Play music and let your children crawl and hop around like spiders. Then encourage them to dance in ever-widening circles as they "spin their webs."

Spin, Spin, Little Spider

Sung to: "Ten Little Indians"

Spin, spin, little spider,
Spin, spin, wider, wider.
Spin, spin, little spider,
Early in the morning.

Dance, dance, little spider,
Dance, dance, dance out wider.
Dance, dance, little spider,
Early in the morning.

Make your web, little spider,
Make your web, wider, wider.
Make your web, little spider,
Early in the morning.

Jean Warren

The Eeensy Weensy Spider

Sung to: "Eensy Weensy Spider"

The eensy weensy spider
Climbed up the water spout.
Down came the rain
And washed the spider out.
Out came the sun
And dried up all the rain.
And the eensy weensy spider
Climbed up the spout again.

Traditional

LANGUAGE IDEA

Show your children a spider in a closed container. Talk about what the spider looks like and how it moves.

SNACK IDEA

Insert pretzel sticks or crunchy Chinese noodles into the sides of prunes to make "spiders."

Little Miss Muffet

Spider Finger Puppets

For each of your children, cut a 2-inch square from black construction paper. Wrap the square snugly around the tip of the child's finger and tape it securely near the top. Cut slits around the bottom of the puppet to make eight legs. Fold the legs out. Let the children use their puppets to act out "Little Miss Muffet" or other spider rhymes.

MOVEMENT

Musical Tuffets

For each of your children, place a pillow or a carpet square on the floor for a "tuffet." Play music and let the children walk around the room. Whenever you stop the music, have each child find a tuffet to sit on.

RHYME

Little Miss Muffet

Little Miss Muffet
Sat on a tuffet,
Eating her curds and whey.
Along came a spider
That down beside her,
And frightened Miss Muffet away.

Traditional

The Miss Muffet Song

Sung to: "Clementine"

I'm Miss Muffet, I'm Miss Muffet,
I'm Miss Muffet now today.
I'm Miss Muffet on a tuffet,
Eating all my curds and whey.

I'm the Spider, I'm the Spider,
I'm the Spider now today.
I'm the Spider just beside her,
I will make her run away.

Lois E. Putnam

Miss Muffett and the Spider

Sung to: "The Mulberry Bush"

Little Miss Muffet went out to play,
Out to play, out to play.
Little Miss Muffet went out to play,
So early in the morning.

She saw a spider and ran away,
Ran away, ran away.
She saw a spider and ran away,
So early in the morning.

Elizabeth McKinnon

LANGUAGE IDEA

Talk about how Miss Muffet was frightened by the spider. Encourage your children to tell about things that frighten them and how they handle their fears.

SNACK IDEA

Serve cottage cheese and talk about the curds.

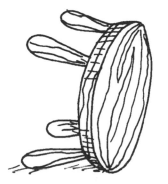

Black

RHYME

My Black Hen

Hickety, pickety,
My black hen,
She lays eggs
For gentlemen.
Sometimes nine,
Sometimes ten,
Hickety, pickety,
My black hen.

Adapted Traditional

HANDS-ON ART

Black Texture Collages

Give each of your children a black posterboard square or a black paper plate. Set out scraps of different-textured black items such as sandpaper, velveteen, yarn, fake fur, and plastic. Let your children brush glue all over their posterboard squares or paper plates. Then have them arrange the textured items on top of the glue to create collages.

MOVEMENT

Stuff the Pillow

Cut a stack of newspapers into squares. Have your children help crumple the squares and stuff them inside a large black trash bag. When the bag is full, close it securely and let the children take turns jumping on their big black "pillow."

SONGS

If You Are Wearing Black

Sung to: "If You're Happy and You Know It"

If you are wearing black,
Pat your back.
If you are wearing black,
Pat your back.
If you are wearing black,
Then please pat your back.
If you are wearing black,
Pat your back.

Janice Bodenstedt

Baa, Baa, Black Sheep

Sung to: "Twinkle, Twinkle, Little Star"

Baa, baa, black sheep,
Have you any wool?
Yes sir, yes sir,
Three bags full.
One for my master,
And one for my dame,
And one for the little boy
Who lives down the lane.
Baa, baa, black sheep,
Have you any wool?
Yes sir, yes sir,
Three bags full.

Adapted Traditional

LANGUAGE IDEA

Select a black teddy bear or other stuffed toy. Make up a story about the animal's adventures.

SNACK IDEA

Serve black olives or licorice sticks.

Pots and Pans

Putting on Lids

Select several different-size pots and pans with lids. Give the pots and pans to your children. Let them remove the lids, mix them up, and then put them back on the appropriate pots and pans.

MOVEMENT

Peas in the Pot

Stand in a circle with your children. Recite the rhyme "Pea Soup" (this page) and let the children take turns jumping into the middle of the circle. At the end of the rhyme, have everyone jump back out again.

RHYME

Pea Soup

One little pea jumped into the pot,
And waited for the soup to get hot.
> *(Cup hand and bend down thumb.)*
Two little peas jumped into the pot,
And waited for the soup to get hot.
> *(Bend down pointer finger.)*
Three little peas jumped into the pot,
And waited for the soup to get hot.
> *(Bend down middle finger.)*
Four little peas jumped into the pot,
And waited for the soup to get hot.
> *(Bend down ring finger.)*
Five little peas jumped into the pot,
And waited for the soup to get hot.
> *(Bend down little finger.)*
Finally, the soup got so very hot,
All the little peas jumped out of the pot!
> *(Quickly open hand.)*

Jean Warren

SONG

Pots and Pans Marching Band

Sung to: "The Muffin Man"

Marching with our pots and pans,
Pots and pans, pots and pans,
Marching with our pots and pans
In our marching band.

Hear us bang our pots and pans,
Pots and pans, pots and pans,
Hear us bang our pots and pans
In our marching band.

As you sing the song, let your children march around the room, banging on pots and pans with wooden spoons.

Elizabeth McKinnon

LANGUAGE IDEA

Let your children take turns placing plastic vegetables or vegetable pictures into a large pot as you tell a story about making stew.

SNACK IDEA

Serve snacks in foil tart pans.

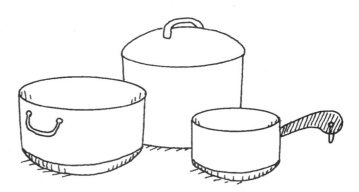

Spoons

HANDS-ON ART

Painting With Spoons

Give each of your children a piece of finger-paint paper or a square cut from a brown paper bag. Pour tempera paint into paint containers and add some salt for texture. Place a small amount of the paint on each child's paper. Then let your children use spoons to push the paint around. Add more paint to the children's papers as needed.

MOVEMENT

Stirring Fun

Have your children pretend to be spoons in a big pot of soup. Let them move around and around, pretending to stir the soup as you recite the rhyme below. Then repeat the rhyme, each time substituting a different food name for *soup*.

Stirring our soup,
Stirring it slow,
Stirring and stirring,
Around we go.

Elizabeth McKinnon

RHYME

My Spoon

I eat and eat
With my spoon, just so.
Eating right
Will help me grow.

Jean Warren

LANGUAGE IDEA

Make a puppet by drawing a face on the bowl of a wooden spoon and tying on a piece of fabric for clothing. Use the spoon puppet to tell a story.

SNACK IDEA

Serve a snack, such as yogurt, and set out different kinds of spoons (a teaspoon, a serving spoon, a plastic spoon, etc.). Let each of your children choose a special spoon to use for eating his or her snack.

SONG

Dancing Spoon

Sung to: "The Muffin Man"

Have you seen my dancing spoon,
Dancing spoon, dancing spoon,
Have you seen my dancing spoon,
As round and round it goes?

Yes, I've seen your dancing spoon,
Dancing spoon, dancing spoon,
Yes, I've seen your dancing spoon,
It dances fast, then slow.

Jean Warren

OCTOBER

Pompons

Pompon Play

Collect various sizes and colors of pompons (available at craft stores) to use for the following activities.

- Place pompons in a plastic dishpan and add scoops, measuring cups, and spoons. Let your children experiment with pouring and "measuring" the pompons.
- Have your children sort pompons by color or by size into the cups of a muffin tin.
- Let your children line up pompons from smallest to largest or from largest to smallest.

MOVEMENT

Dancing Pompons

Have your children wear hats with pompons on the tops and pretend to be Dancing Pompons. Play music and let the children dance around on tiptoe, bounce gently up and down, then roll around on the floor.

RHYME

Pretty Pompons

Pretty pompons here and there,
Pretty pompons everywhere.
Red and yellow, green and blue,
Some for me and some for you!

Susan Burbridge

SONG

Found a Pompon

Sung to: "Clementine"

Found a pompon,
Found a pompon,
Found a pompon just now.
Found a pompon on the floor,
On the floor just now.

Took that pompon,
Took that pompon,
Took that pompon just now.
Then I put it in a basket,
In a basket just now.

Each time you sing the song, substitute appropriate phrases for *on the floor* and *in a basket*.

Elizabeth McKinnon

LANGUAGE IDEA

Make a puppet by gluing a pompon to the top of a pencil or a craft stick and attaching plastic moving eyes. Use the pompon puppet to tell a story.

SNACK IDEA

Serve melon balls in a variety of kinds and colors.

The Moon

HANDS-ON ART

Moon Pictures

Select a piece of white construction paper for each of your children. On each paper, use a white crayon to draw and color in a circle for a moon. (Be sure to press down hard with the crayon while coloring.) Then let each child brush thinned black tempera paint over his or her paper to reveal the moon glowing in the black night sky.

MOVEMENT

Dancing Moonbeams

Let your children pretend to be moonbeams dancing around the room. As they dance, guide them with statements such as these: "I see a little moonbeam touching the floor. I see another little moonbeam touching the wall. Now one little moonbeam is touching the table and another one is touching the chair."

RHYME

Hey, Diddle, Diddle

Hey, diddle, diddle,
The cat and the fiddle,
The cow jumped
Over the moon.
The little dog laughed
To see such sport,
And the dish ran away
With the spoon.

Traditional

It Is Nighttime

Sung to: "Clementine"

It is nighttime, see the moon,
It is right there overhead.
Now, that means just one thing,
It is time to go to bed.

Gayle Bittinger

Moon Glow, Moon Glow

Sung to: "Twinkle, Twinkle, Little Star"

Moon glow, moon glow in the night.
Moon glow, moon glow, gentle light.
How I love to see you there,
Softly shining everywhere!
Moon glow, moon glow in the night.
Moon glow, moon glow, gentle light.

Margaret Timmons

LANGUAGE IDEA

Use felt shapes on a flannelboard to tell the nursery rhyme "Hey, Diddle, Diddle" (page 52).

SNACK IDEA

Serve round rice cakes at snacktime. Let your children spread on softened cream cheese, if desired.

Owls

Where Is Little Owl?

Choose one of your children to be Little Owl. While the other children close their eyes, help Little Owl find a hiding place. When the other children open their eyes, have Little Owl make hooting sounds. Have the other children listen carefully and try to guess where Little Owl is hiding. When Little Owl is found, choose another child to take his or her place and start the game again.

MOVEMENT

Owls in a Tree

Let your children pretend to be owls sitting in a tree. Have them look all around by moving their heads from side to side and blinking their big "owl eyes." Then have them flap their wings and "fly" around the room, making hooting sounds, before returning to their places in the tree.

RHYME

Wise Old Owl

Wise old owl
In the tree,
Whoo-oo are you winking at?
    (Wink eye.)
Is it me?

Jean Warren

SONG

Little Owl

Sung to: "This Old Man"

Little owl, in the tree,
He is winking down at me.
With a wink, wink, wink, wink,
All through the night,
Little owl is quite a sight!

Little owl, in the tree,
He is hooting down at me.
With a hoot, hoot, hoot, hoot,
All through the night,
Little owl is quite a sight!

Jean Warren

LANGUAGE IDEA

Read or tell an owl story. Whenever your children hear the word *owl*, have them make hooting sounds.

SNACK IDEA

Give your children small celery stalk "trees" stuffed with peanut butter. Let each child stick a raisin "owl" on his or her tree.

Cats

HANDS-ON ART

Cat Collage

Place a large piece of paper on a low table or on the floor. Give your children pictures of cats cut or torn from magazines. Help the children brush glue on the paper. Then let them place the cat pictures on top of the glue to make a collage. Hang the collage on a wall at the children's eye level and encourage them to discuss the different cat pictures.

MOVEMENT

Cat Moves

Have your children pretend to be cats sleeping on the floor. Have them wake up, stretch, then pretend to wash their faces with their paws. Hold a pretend toy on a string above the Cats and let them jump and swat at it. When the Cats become sleepy, have them roll over, curl up, and go back to sleep again.

RHYME

Soft Kitty, Warm Kitty

Soft kitty, warm kitty,
Little ball of fur.
> *(Form fist with one hand.)*

Pretty kitty, sleepy kitty,
Purr, purr, purr.
> *(Stroke fist with other hand.)*

Adapted Traditional

I'm a Little Kitten

Sung to: "I'm a Little Teapot"

I'm a little kitten,
Soft and furry.
I'll be your friend,
So don't you worry.
Right up on your lap
I like to hop.
I'll purr, purr, purr,
And never stop.

Betty Silkunas

My Kitten

Sung to: "Sing a Song of Sixpence"

I have a little kitten,
She's black and white and gray.
When I try to cuddle her,
She always wants to play.
So I drag a piece of yarn
Across the kitchen floor.
She thinks it is a little mouse
To chase right out the door.

Elizabeth Vollrath

LANGUAGE IDEA

Using a toy cat as a prop, tell a story about a cat or a kitten. Encourage your children to imitate the cat in the story when it mews, hisses, and purrs.

SNACK IDEA

Serve foods that cats like such as milk and tuna fish.

Scarecrows

Hanging Scarecrow

Let your children help you make a hanging scarecrow for your room. Give them squares of newspaper to crumple and stuff into a small brown paper bag. Close the bag with a twist tie, turn it upside down, and draw a face on one side with felt-tip markers. Tape the bag securely to the top part of a coat hanger. Put an old shirt on the hanger, add a scarf, and the scarecrow is ready to hang. If desired, let the children stuff more crumpled newspaper into the sleeves and body of the scarecrow's shirt to add fullness.

RHYME

Scarecrow, Scarecrow

Scarecrow, scarecrow,
What does he see,
As he stands alone
By the old oak tree?
A bird and some corn,
That's what he sees,
As he stands alone
By the old oak tree.

Repeat, letting your children substitute other words for *bird* and *corn*.

Jean Warren

MOVEMENT

Scarecrow and Crows

Stand in the middle of an open area with your arms at your sides. Let your children walk around you, pretending to be crows. Whenever you hold your arms out like a scarecrow's, have the children "fly away." Whenever you lower your arms, have the children come back and walk around you again.

Did You Ever See a Scarecrow?

Sung to: "Did You Ever See a Lassie?"

Did you ever see a scarecrow,
A scarecrow, a scarecrow,
> *(Stand with arms stiffly out at sides.)*
Did you ever see a scarecrow
Bend this way and that?
> *(Bend to one side, then the other.)*
Bend this way and that way,
Bend this way and that way.
> *(Continue bending.)*
Did you ever see a scarecrow
Bend this way and that?
> *(Bend to one side, then the other.)*

Did you ever see a scarecrow,
A scarecrow, a scarecrow,
> *(Stand with arms stiffly out at sides.)*
Did you ever see a scarecrow
Wave this way and that?
> *(Wave one hand, then the other.)*
Wave this way and that way,
Wave this way and that way.
> *(Continue waving hands.)*
Did you ever see a scarecrow
Wave this way and that?
> *(Wave one hand, then the other.)*

Elizabeth McKinnon

LANGUAGE IDEA

Cut the parts of a scarecrow out of felt. Let your children make up a story about a scarecrow as they put the felt shapes together on a flannelboard.

SNACK IDEA

Serve corn on the cob, cut into manageable lengths, with butter or margarine.

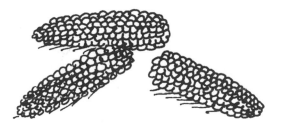

Pumpkins

Pumpkins Big and Small

Collect small and large pumpkins. Let your children divide the pumpkins into two groups by size. Then help them count the number of pumpkins in each group. Mix up the pumpkins and let the children sort them again.

MOVEMENT

Pumpkin Roll

Have your children pretend to be pumpkins. Let them roll around on the floor as you recite the following rhyme.

Pumpkins, pumpkins
On the ground,
Rolling, rolling
All around.
See them rolling
Down the hill—
Now they stop
And lie so still.

Elizabeth McKinnon

RHYME

Pumpkin, Pumpkin

Pumpkin, pumpkin,
Sitting on the wall,
   (Sit on floor.)
Pumpkin, pumpkin,
Tip and fall.
   (Fall to one side.)

Pumpkin, pumpkin,
Rolling down the street,
   (Roll on floor.)
Pumpkin, pumpkin,
Trick-or-treat!

Author Unknown

Display a small pumpkin for your children to touch, examine, and discuss. Then cut open the pumpkin and talk about what is inside.

SNACK IDEA

Cook pieces of fresh pumpkin and let your children help mash them. Use the mashed pumpkin to make pumpkin pie.

SONG

Pumpkin on the Ground

Sung to: "Twinkle, Twinkle, Little Star"

Pumpkin, pumpkin on the ground,
How'd you get so big and round?
You started as a seed so small.
Now you are a great round ball.
Pumpkin, pumpkin on the ground,
How'd you get so big and round?

Diane Thom

Pumpkin Patch

HANDS-ON SCIENCE

Visiting a Pumpkin Patch

Arrange a field trip with your children to a pumpkin farm. Before you go, discuss how pumpkins grow, using a set of sequence picture cards that include a seed in the ground, a sprout, a flowering vine, and a vine with pumpkins on it. When you visit the farm, point out the different parts of a pumpkin plant. Then let your children help choose one or more pumpkins to take back with you.

MOVEMENT

Pumpkin Patch Game

Cut pumpkin shapes out of orange construction paper. Hide the shapes around the room and let your children search for them. If desired, give your children plastic pumpkins to use for carrying the pumpkin shapes that they find.

RHYME

Pumpkins Are Growing

Pumpkins are growing
On the ground.
   (Point downward.)
Look at all the pumpkins
Orange and round!
   (Form circle with arms.)

Diane Thom

In the Pumpkin Patch

Sung to: "The Paw-Paw Patch"

There are pumpkins on the ground,
There are pumpkins to be found,
There are pumpkins all around,
Way down yonder in the pumpkin patch.

Gayle Bittinger

I Planted a Seed

Sung to: "Little White Duck"

I planted a seed,
Oh, so very small.
It grew and it grew,
But it still wasn't tall.
Then a bud appeared one day,
And then a pumpkin came to stay.
Now I have a pumpkin round
Growing on the ground.
Pumpkin round.

Gayle Bittinger

LANGUAGE IDEA

Make pumpkin finger puppets. Use them to tell a story about a pumpkin family in a pumpkin patch.

SNACK IDEA

Serve pumpkin bread or pumpkin muffins.

Peter, Peter, Pumpkin Eater

In the Pumpkin Shell

Find an orange plastic pumpkin. Inside the pumpkin, place several orange items such as a crayon, a block, a mitten, and a napkin. Let your children take turns removing the items from the pumpkin, naming each one, then putting all the items back into the pumpkin again.

Peter, Peter, Pumpkin Eater

Peter, Peter, pumpkin eater,
Had a mouse but couldn't keep her.
He put her in a pumpkin shell,
And there he kept her very well.

Adapted Traditional

Where Are the Mice?

Recite the adapted rhyme "Peter, Peter, Pumpkin Eater" (this page). Then play the following game. Let your children pretend to be Mice while you take the part of Peter. As you cover your eyes, have the children scurry around the room and find places to hide. When you open your eyes, walk around looking for the Mice. Each time a Mouse is found, let him or her join in the search for the remaining Mice. Continue until all the Mice have been found.

Variation: Let older children take turns playing the role of Peter.

LANGUAGE IDEA

Recite "Peter, Peter, Pumpkin Eater" (page 64) with your children, each time substituting a different animal name for *mouse*. Let the children act out the rhyme by placing toy animals inside a plastic pumpkin.

SONG

Peter, Peter, Pumpkin Head

Sung to: "Twinkle, Twinkle, Little Star"

Peter, Peter,
Pumpkin head,
Eats pumpkin pies
And pumpkin bread,
Pumpkin muffins,
Pumpkin cake,
And pumpkin cookies
Freshly baked.
Peter, Peter,
Pumpkin head,
Full of pumpkins,
You're well fed!

Diane Thom

SNACK IDEA

Wrap snack foods in foil or plastic wrap. Place them in a plastic pumpkin for serving at snacktime.

Orange

Finger Painting With Orange

Give each of your children a piece of white butcher paper or construction paper. In the center of each paper, place a spoonful of orange finger paint. Let the children use their hands and fingers to create designs with the paint. When they have finished, allow their papers to dry. Then cut the papers into pumpkin shapes (or orange shapes) and display them around the room.

MOVEMENT

Orange Streamer Dance

Cut orange crepe-paper streamers into pieces. Tape the pieces to your children's wrists. Then play music and let the children dance around the room, waving and twirling their orange streamers.

RHYME

Orange

I love
The color orange.
Oh yes, oh yes,
I do!
It's the color
Of orange juice,
And carrots
And pumpkins too.

Jean Warren

Orange, Orange, Orange

Sung to: "Three Blind Mice"

Orange, orange, orange.
Orange, orange, orange.
What is orange? What is orange?
An orange, a cantaloupe, and a peach,
A pumpkin, a goldfish, and cheddar cheese,
The carrot that my little rabbit eats,
They all are orange.

Diane Thom

An Orange Crayon

Sung to: "Mary Had a Little Lamb"

I have an orange crayon,
Orange crayon,
Orange crayon.
I have an orange crayon,
Watch me draw a pumpkin.

I have an orange crayon,
Orange crayon,
Orange crayon.
I have an orange crayon,
Watch me draw a carrot.

Substitute the names of other orange
things for *pumpkin* and *carrot*.

Jean Warren

LANGUAGE IDEA

Let your children place orange
objects in a box. Incorporate the
names of the objects as you make
up an "orange story."

SNACK IDEA

Serve orange foods such as carrots, cheese, and peaches.

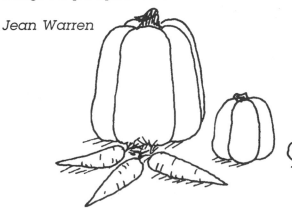

Oranges

Sensing Oranges

Give your children oranges to touch and examine. Encourage them to tell what the oranges look like and how they feel. Peel one of the oranges and ask the children to listen to the soft sound. Then give an orange section to each child. How do the orange sections smell? How do they taste?

MOVEMENT

Picking Oranges

Place oranges on one side of the room. Put a basket on the opposite side of the room and have your children stand beside it. Let the children run across the room, "pick" the oranges as if from a tree, then run back and place the oranges in the basket. Continue until all the oranges have been picked.

RHYME

I'm a Juicy Orange

I'm a juicy orange
Round as you please,
(Form circle with arms.)
A big juicy orange
Waiting for a squeeze.
(Squeeze hands together.)
So if you happen
To come my way,
(Point to other person.)
Give me a hug—
You'll make my day!
(Hug self.)

Jean Warren

What Does an Orange Look Like?

Sung to: "The Mulberry Bush"

What does an orange look like,
Orange look like, orange look like?
What does an orange look like?
It looks round and orange.

What does an orange feel like,
Orange feel like, orange feel like?
What does an orange feel like?
It feels a little bumpy.

What does an orange sound like,
Orange sound like, orange sound like?
What does an orange sound like?
Listen carefully.

What does an orange smell like,
Orange smell like, orange smell like?
What does an orange smell like?
It smells nice and sweet.

What does an orange taste like,
Orange taste like, orange taste like?
What does an orange taste like?
It tastes oh, so yummy!

Kathy Gonion

LANGUAGE IDEA

Make up a story about a rolling orange and its adventures. Use a real orange for a prop.

SNACK IDEA

Let your children help squeeze oranges to make orange juice. Serve with orange slices for the children to taste and compare with the juice.

Jack-O'-Lanterns

Felt Jack-O'-Lanterns

Cut one or two large pumpkin shapes out of orange felt. Use black felt to make four or more different-shaped noses, mouths, and sets of eyes. Place the felt pumpkins on a table or on the floor. Let your children arrange the facial features on the pumpkins to create different jack-o'-lantern faces.

MOVEMENT

Jack-O'-Lantern Parade

Make a paper headband for each of your children. On the front of each headband, attach a small construction-paper pumpkin shape on which you have drawn a jack-o'-lantern face. Fasten the head-bands around the children's foreheads. Then play music and let the children march around the room in a Jack-O'-Lantern Parade.

RHYME

I'm a Little Pumpkin

I'm a little pumpkin, look at me,
I'm round and cute as I can be.
 (Bend arms out at sides.)
Carve a face and add a candle bright,
I'll glow and glow all through the night.
 (Form circle with arms and smile.)

Deborah A. Roessel

Picked a Pumpkin

Sung to: "Clementine"

Picked a pumpkin,
Picked a pumpkin
That was growing
On a vine.
Then I carved
A jack-o'-lantern,
And it turned out
Just fine.

Sue Brown

I'm a Jack-O'-Lantern

Sung to: "I'm a Little Teapot"

I'm a jack-o'-lantern,
Look at me.
I'm as happy
As I can be.
Put a candle in
And light the light.
Don't be frightened,
It's Halloween night!

Betty Ruth Baker

LANGUAGE IDEA

Dim the lights and tell a story by
the light of a jack-o'-lantern.

SNACK IDEA

Make cheese sandwiches that
have jack-o'-lantern faces cut out
of the top slices of bread.

Pumpkin Faces

Pumpkin Face Match-Up

Select six to eight white index cards and divide them into pairs. Draw different matching pumpkin faces on each pair of cards. Mix up the cards and give them to your children. Let them take turns finding the matching pairs of pumpkin faces.

MOVEMENT

Where Is Pumpkin?

Sing the song below with your children and let them act out the movements indicated.

Sung to: "Frere Jacques"

Where is pumpkin?
Where is pumpkin?
    (Crouch low.)
Here I am!
Here I am!
    (Jump up.)
I am round and orange.
    (Form circle with arms.)
See my funny face.
    (Make a face.)
Now you don't.
Now you don't.
    (Crouch low and hide face.)

Author Unknown

RHYME

Pumpkin Faces Everywhere

Pumpkin faces
In strange places
Everywhere I go.
Some are happy,
Some are sad,
Some are in a row.

Pumpkin faces
In strange places
All around the town.
Some up high,
Some down low,
Sitting on the ground.

Jean Warren

SONGS

Pumpkin Faces

Sung to: "Twinkle, Twinkle, Little Star"

Pumpkin faces here and there,
Pumpkin faces everywhere.
Faces ready for Halloween,
Funniest faces we've ever seen.
Pumpkin faces here and there,
Pumpkin faces everywhere.

Elizabeth McKinnon

Little Pumpkin

Sung to: "I'm a Little Teapot"

I'm a little pumpkin,
Orange and round.
When I'm sad,
My face wears a frown.
But when I am happy
And all aglow,
Watch my smile
Just grow and grow!

Barbara Hasson

LANGUAGE IDEA

Draw faces on orange construction-paper pumpkin shapes and attach the shapes to the tops of craft sticks. Let your children use the pumpkin puppets to tell stories.

SNACK IDEA

Let your children spread soft orange cheese on round crackers and add raisins for eyes, noses, and mouths.

Feelings

HANDS-ON LEARNING GAME

Sorting Out Feelings

Select two paper plates. Draw a happy face on one plate and a sad face on the other. Cut out magazine pictures of people who look happy and people who look sad. Place the paper-plate faces on a low table or on the floor. Help your children sort the pictures into two groups by placing the happy-looking people around the happy-face plate and the sad-looking people around the sad-face plate.

MOVEMENT

Be a Bear

Ask each of your children to be a bear (a Melissa Bear, an Andrew Bear, a Jessica Bear, etc.). Have the children roll and play like happy bears, then stomp around and growl like angry bears. Continue in a similar way, having the children act out other feelings such as hunger, sadness, or sleepiness.

RHYME

I Look in the Mirror

I look in the mirror,
　　(Pretend to look in mirror.)
And what do I see?
I see a happy face
　　(Smile.)
Smiling at me.

I look in the mirror,
　　(Pretend to look in mirror.)
And what do I see?
I see a sad face
　　(Frown.)
Frowning at me.

Adapted Traditional

I'm a Happy Face

Sung to: "I'm a Little Teapot"

I'm a happy face,
Just watch me grin.
I've a great big smile
From my forehead to my chin.
  (Smile.)
But when I'm upset
And things are bad,
Then my happy face
Turns to sad.
  (Frown.)

Jean Warren

I'll Hug You

Sung to: "The Farmer in the Dell"

I'll hug you
When you're sad,
I'll hug you
When you're glad,
I'll hug you
When you're feeling scared,
I'll hug you
When you're mad.

Betty Silkunas

LANGUAGE IDEA

Draw a happy face on one side of a paper plate and a sad face on the other side. Use the plate as a puppet for telling stories.

SNACK IDEA

Serve a nutritious "feel good" snack such as fruit, juice, or vegetables with a yogurt dip.

Pizzas

HANDS-ON COOKING

Making Pizzas

Let your children help make mini-pizzas. Brown English muffin halves under the broiler. When cool, give one half to each child with a spoonful of pizza sauce on it. Let the children spread the sauce all over their muffin halves and then sprinkle on shredded cheese. Give them bits of cooked meat and vegetables to add to their pizzas for toppings. Broil the pizzas for 2 to 3 minutes or until the cheese is soft and bubbly. Allow the pizzas to cool slightly before serving.

Variation: Let your children use sliced black olives to make jack-o'-lantern faces on their pizzas.

Hint: To make sure each child is served his or her own pizza, slip a foil strip with the child's name etched on it under the pizza before broiling.

MOVEMENT

Musical Pizzas

Find one cardboard pizza round for each of your children. Place the cardboard circles on the floor. Play music and have your children walk around the circles. Whenever you stop the music, have everyone stop walking and find a cardboard circle to sit on. Continue the game as long as interest lasts.

RHYME

Pizza Treat

It's round and made of dough,
Topped with sauce and cheese just so.
   (Form circle with hands.)
It's a big round treat
Filled with vegetables and meat.
   (Rub tummy.)
It's a pizza cooked just right.
Are you ready? Have a bite!
   (Pretend to eat pizza.)

Diane Thom

I Wish I Were a Pepperoni Pizza

Sung to: "The Oscar Mayer Theme Song"

Oh, I wish I were a pepperoni pizza,
That is what I'd truly like to be.
For if I were a pepperoni pizza,
Everyone would be in love with me!

Repeat, each time substituting a different
pizza name for *pepperoni*.

Jean Warren

Pizza Song

Sung to: "If You're Happy and You Know It"

If you want to eat some pizza,
Raise your hand.
If you want to eat some pizza,
Raise your hand.
If you like bubbly cheese,
Then just say, "Pizza please!"
If you want to eat some pizza,
Raise your hand.

Jean Warren

LANGUAGE IDEA

Cut pizza topping shapes out of
felt. Let your children arrange
them on a red felt circle as you
talk about how to make a pizza.

SNACK IDEA

After doing the activity Making
Pizzas (page 76), place your
children's warm mini-pizzas in a
pizza box and "deliver" them to
the snack table.

Triangles

HANDS-ON ART

Triangle Collages

Cut small triangles out of colored construction paper, tissue paper, wallpaper, and gift wrap. Give each of your children a piece of white construction paper. Have the children brush glue all over their papers. Then let them arrange the triangles on top of the glue any way they wish to make collages.

MOVEMENT

Triangle Walk

Use pieces of masking tape to make large outlines of triangles on the floor. Let your children take turns walking, crawling, or hopping around the edges of the shapes.

RHYME

The Triangle

The triangle is a simple shape,
I think you will agree.
Count its sides and corners,
And you will find just three.

Author Unknown

The Triangle Song

Sung to: "Pop! Goes the Weasel"

I am a small triangle,
I have three sides, you see.
I also have three corners.
They're just right for me!

Rita J. Galloway

LANGUAGE IDEA

With your children, manipulate triangular paper shapes or blocks to make new shapes. Talk about how the new shapes are formed and what they look like.

SNACK IDEA

Serve triangular toast slices, cheese slices, or sandwich halves.

A Lovely Triangle

Sung to: "You Are My Sunshine"

I'm a triangle,
A lovely triangle,
I have three sides,
They're all the same.
I have three corners,
Three lovely corners,
I'm a triangle,
That's my name.

Rita J. Galloway

Orange and Black

Orange and Black Fun

Cut seasonal shapes out of orange and black felt (pumpkins, haystacks, bats, cats, etc.). Place the shapes in a plastic pumpkin or other container. Let your children take turns removing the shapes from the pumpkin and placing them on a flannelboard. Then help the children group all the orange shapes on one side of the flannelboard and all the black shapes on the other side.

MOVEMENT

Pompon Shake

Cut 2-foot lengths of orange and black crepe-paper streamers. Make a pompon for each of your children by placing four streamers one on top of the other, tying them together in the middle, then fluffing out the ends. Let the children shake the pompons up, down, and all around as you play music.

RHYME

Orange and Black

Orange and black
Here and there,
Orange and black
Everywhere.
When orange and black
Can be seen,
We know it's time
For Halloween!

Elizabeth McKinnon

LANGUAGE IDEA

Use orange and black finger puppets to tell a Halloween story.

SNACK IDEA

Serve orange cheese with black raisins or prunes.

SONG

If You See an Orange Pumpkin

Sung to: "If You're Happy and You Know It"

If you see an orange pumpkin,
Touch it now.
If you see an orange pumpkin,
Touch it now.
If you see an orange pumpkin,
If you see an orange pumpkin,
If you see an orange pumpkin,
Touch it now.

If you see a black crayon,
Bring it here.
If you see a black crayon,
Bring it here.
If you see a black crayon,
If you see a black crayon,
If you see a black crayon,
Bring it here.

Continue with similar verses about orange and black objects placed around your room.

Marjorie Debowy

Stickers

Sticker Collages

Give each of your children a piece of construction paper and an assortment of stickers. Help the children remove the stickers from the backings. Then let them attach their stickers to their papers any way they wish.

Variation: To make the stickers "reusable," let your children create their collages on sheets of waxed paper instead of construction paper.

MOVEMENT

Sticker Fingers

Attach a sticker to one of each child's index fingers. Then give directions such as these: "Hold your sticker high. Touch your sticker to the floor. Move your sticker around in a circle. Dance your sticker in the air."

RHYME

Sticker Pals

Make Sticker Pals by attaching a sticker to each index finger.

Where's my Sticker Pal?
Where's my Sticker Pal?
  (Hide fingers behind back.)
Here I am!
Here I am!
  (Bring fingers forward.)
How are you today, Pal?
Very well, I thank you.
  (Nod fingers at each other.)
Run away.
Run away.
  (Hide fingers behind back.)

Adapted Traditional

SONG

Stick Our Stickers

Sung to: "Row, Row, Row Your Boat"

Stick, stick, stick our stickers,
Stick them all around.
Let's count the stickers we have stuck,
How many can be found?

As you sing the song, attach stickers to a
piece of waxed paper. After counting, remove the stickers, then sing and stick again.

Ellen Bedford

LANGUAGE IDEA

Draw a story background on a
piece of paper. Give each of your
children a sticker to attach to the
background as you tell the story.

SNACK IDEA

For each of your children, attach
two identical stickers back to
back near the top of a plastic
straw. Let the children use their
decorated straws for drinking
milk or juice.

Costumes

Costume Fun

Place a box of dress-up clothes and hats on the floor near a wall mirror. Encourage each of your children to dress up by reciting the rhyme below as he or she tries on each new "costume."

Mirror, mirror
On the wall,
Who is the silliest
One of all?

Ellen Javernick

MOVEMENT

Costume Parade

Help each of your children dress in a simple costume such as a firefighter hat and boots or a princess cape and crown. Then play music and let the children parade around the room.

RHYME

I Look in the Mirror

I look in the mirror
And what do I see?
I see a cowgirl
Looking at me.

Repeat the rhyme with each of your children, substituting the name of his or her costume for *cowgirl*.

Adapted Traditional

LANGUAGE IDEA

LANGUAGE IDEA

Hold up different parts of a costume, such as a mask, a hat, and a cape, and let your children name them.

SNACK IDEA

Let your children wear simple costumes when they come to the snack table.

SONGS

The Costume Song

Sung to: "London Bridge"

Michael has a costume on,

Costume on, costume on.

Michael has a costume on.

He's a pirate.

Repeat, each time substituting the name of one of your children for *Michael* and the name of his or her costume for *pirate*.

Elizabeth McKinnon

A Special Costume

Sung to: "The Oscar Mayer Theme Song"

Oh, I like to dress up
In a special costume,
Then parade around
For everyone to see.
For when I dress up
In a special costume,
I can be whatever
I want to be.

Jean Warren

Pretending

HANDS-ON DRAMATIC PLAY

Pretending Fun

Lead your children in various pretend activities such as throwing a ball, painting a picture, or holding and rocking a baby. Continue by asking them to show how they would walk upstairs, drive a car, or drink a glass of water. Encourage the children to show you other things they can pretend to do.

RHYME

Let's Pretend

Let's pretend that we are kittens
  (Do actions as rhyme indicates.)
Playing with some yarn.
Let's pretend that we are ponies
Prancing round the barn.
Let's pretend that we are caterpillars
Crawling on a limb.
Let's pretend that we are fishes
And swim, swim, swim.

Elizabeth McKinnon

MOVEMENT

Animal Pretending

Act out the movements of a familiar animal such as a puppy. Get down on all fours, pretend to wag your tail, and give a few barks. Have your children guess what animal you are pretending to be. Then invite them to join you in pretending to be that animal. Start the game again by choosing another animal and acting out its movements.

Let's Pretend to Be Elephants

Sung to: "The Mulberry Bush"

Let's pretend to be elephants,
Elephants, elephants,
Let's pretend to be elephants
And stomp around this way.

Let's pretend to be kitty cats,
Kitty cats, kitty cats,
Let's pretend to be kitty cats
And roll around this way.

Let's pretend to be little birds,
Little birds, little birds,
Let's pretend to be little birds
And fly around this way.

Additional verses: Let's pretend to be falling leaves and twirl around this way; Let's pretend to be little cars and drive around this way; Let's pretend to be rubber balls and bounce around this way; etc.

Elizabeth McKinnon

LANGUAGE IDEA

Tell a familiar story, using imaginary props and pretending to act out the movements. Encourage your children to join you in the pretending.

SNACK IDEA

Let your children pretend to eat a favorite food before you serve them their snack.

PRETENDING ▪ OCTOBER ▪ 87

Parade Fun

Parade Floats

Set out several cardboard boxes to use for floats. Let your children help decorate the boxes by coloring on designs with crayons, felt-tip markers, or paint. If desired, let them also help glue on seasonal paper shapes and crepe-paper streamers. Tie thick yarn handles to the fronts of the boxes. Then let your children place stuffed animals in the decorated Parade Floats and pull them around the room.

MOVEMENT

Marching Practice

Find a drum to hold and ask your children to line up behind you. As you march around the room, beating on the drum, have the children march along behind you, lifting their knees high and keeping their backs and shoulders straight. Vary the tempo of the drum beats as you march.

RHYME

We March Along

We march along,
We march along,
We lift our feet
High off the ground.
We march and sing
A happy song,
As we go
A-marching on.

Diana Nazaruk

In Our Big Parade

Sung to: "The Mulberry Bush"

See the teddy bear march along,
March along, march along,
See the teddy bear march along
In our big parade.

Let each of your children choose a toy
to hold. Then sing a verse of the song
for each child as you parade with the
children around the room.

Elizabeth McKinnon

March Along

Sung to: "Row, Row, Row Your Boat"

March, march, march along,
March along today.
We'll march along
And sing this song,
Then march the other way.

March, march, march along,
Marching all around.
We'll march along
And sing this song,
Then stop and all sit down.

Jean Warren

LANGUAGE IDEA

When your children are getting
ready to parade, ask questions
such as these: "Who will be at the
front of our parade? Who will be
at the back? Who will be in the
middle?"

SNACK IDEA

Let your children march in a
parade to the snack table.

The Woods

A Walk in the Woods

Take your children on a nature hike in a wooded area. Point out the different kinds of trees and let the children touch the bark. Do some of the trees have leaves? Do some have needles? Bring a bag along on your hike for holding nature items, such as leaves, seeds, or pinecones, that the children find.

Extension: Let your children help sort and display their nature items when you return from your walk.

MOVEMENT

Trees in the Woods

Have your children stand in an open area, pretending to be trees growing in the woods. Encourage them to stretch their arms up over their heads like branches. Pretend to be the wind. As you move through the woods, lightly touch each "tree" and have it begin to bend and sway its branches. Continue until all the trees in the woods are swaying back and forth.

RHYME

Tree Friends

Deep in the woods
With trees so tall,
> *(Stretch arms high.)*
I feel so little,
So very small.
> *(Make self small.)*

I love to look up
And see the trees bend.
> *(Look upward.)*
I know they're saying,
"Let's all be friends."
> *(Hug self.)*

Jean Warren

On a flannelboard, hide felt forest animal shapes under a felt tree shape. As you take out each animal shape, incorporate it into a story.

SNACK IDEA

Serve broccoli floret "trees," either raw or cooked.

SONG

Trees, Trees

Sung to: "Row, Row, Row Your Boat"

Trees, trees in the woods,
Growing oh, so tall.
Some have needles,
Some have leaves.
We just love them all!

Elizabeth McKinnon

Little Red Riding Hood

HANDS-ON LEARNING GAME

Cookies in the Basket

Select several cookie cutters, trace around them on brown poster-board, and cut out the shapes. Place the posterboard "cookies" in a basket. Let your children take turns removing the cookies, naming the shapes, then putting the cookies back into the basket again.

Variation: Help your children count the cookies as they put them in and take them out of the basket.

MOVEMENT

Going to Grandma's

Set out the basket and cookie shapes from the Cookies in the Basket activity (this page). Let your children take turns putting the cookies into the basket, carrying them across the room to "Grandma's house," then bringing them back again for the next child. Continue until everyone has had a turn.

RHYME

Red Riding Hood

There once was a little girl
Dressed in red
Who made some cookies
So good.
She took them to
Her grandmother's house.
Her name was
Red Riding Hood.

Elizabeth McKinnon

SONG

Little Red Riding Hood

Sung to: "Row, Row, Row Your Boat"

Little Red Riding Hood
Went walking through the woods.
She took some cookies
To Grandma's house.
Mmmm, they were so good!

Elizabeth McKinnon

LANGUAGE IDEA

Read or tell a simplified version of "Little Red Riding Hood."

SNACK IDEA

Wrap snack foods in foil or plastic and serve them from a basket.

Cookies

Decorating Cookies

Give each of your children a
large cookie shape cut out of
brown construction paper or
posterboard. Set out glue, brushes,
and scraps of colorful paper. Have
your children tear the paper scraps
into small pieces. Then let them
brush glue all over their cookie
shapes and scatter the paper
pieces on top of the glue for
"cookie sprinkles."

MOVEMENT

Cookie Roll-Out

Find a lightweight, rolled-up
sleeping bag (or roll up a small
blanket or foam pad and tie it
with string). Have your children
lie on the floor any way they
wish, pretending to be cookies.
Then use the sleeping bag like
a rolling pin to lightly "roll out"
each of the cookies in turn.

RHYME

Five Little Cookies

Five little cookies
With frosting galore,
Mother ate the white one,
Then there were four.

Four little cookies,
Two and two, you see,
Father ate the green one,
Then there were three.

Three little cookies,
But before I knew,
Sister ate the yellow one,
Then there were two.

Two little cookies,
Oh, what fun!
Brother ate the brown one,
Then there was one.

One little cookie,
Watch me run!
I ate the red one,
Then there were none.

Adapted Traditional

SONGS

I Love Cookies

Sung to: "Alouette"

I love cookies, I love cookies,
I love cookies, thick and thin.
I love cookies in my tum,
I love cookies, yum, yum, yum.
In my tum, yum, yum, yum—oh,
I love cookies, I love cookies,
I love cookies, thick and thin.

Gayle Bittinger

The Cookie Cook

Sung to: "Three Blind Mice"

I am a cookie cook,
A super cookie cook.
I make cookies all day,
In each and every way.
Square and thin and fat and round,
Piled on a plate in a great big mound,
So good I eat them by the pound.
I am a cookie cook.

Kathleen Cubley

LANGUAGE IDEA

Cut cookie shapes out of white, green, yellow, brown, and red felt. Use the shapes on a flannelboard as you recite "Five Little Cookies" (page 96).

SNACK IDEA

Let your children help make cookies for snacktime. Or give them plain cookies to decorate before eating.

Capes

Magic Capes

Set out a variety of capes for your children to try on. Let the children pretend to be different characters, such as kings, queens, magicians, or superheroes, and act out those characters' movements.

Variation: If capes are not available, safety-pin large square scarves or squares of lightweight fabric to the shoulders of the children's shirts.

MOVEMENT

Cape Moves

Help your children dress in capes. Or show them how to hold large square scarves over their shoulders like capes. Then play music and let the children run, fly, dance, and twirl around the room.

RHYME

The Caped Crusader

I'm known as the Caped Crusader,
I fly across the land.
If you need help, just holler,
I'll come and give you a hand!

Let your children pretend to be caped superheroes as you recite the rhyme.

Jean Warren

SONGS

I Love to Wear a Cape

Sung to: "Did You Ever See a Lassie?"

Oh, I love to wear a cape,
A cape, a cape.
Oh, I love to wear a cape
And fly around.
I zoom and zoom
Around the room.
Oh, I love to wear a cape
And fly around.

Jean Warren

Twirling, Swirling

Sung to: "Frere Jacques"

Twirling, swirling; twirling, swirling,
Round and round, round and round.
I can make my cape twirl,
I can make my cape swirl,
Round and round, round and round.

Gayle Bittinger

LANGUAGE IDEA

Wear a "story cape" when you read or tell a story to your children.

SNACK IDEA

Let your children wear capes when they come to the snack table.

Face Parts

HANDS-ON LEARNING GAME

Magnetic Face Game

Cut a large circle out of heavy paper to represent a face. Cover the circle with clear self-stick paper and glue it to an old non-aluminum baking sheet. Cut eye, nose, mouth, ear, and hair shapes out of construction paper. Cover the shapes with clear self-stick paper and attach pieces of magnetic strip to the backs. To play, let your children take turns placing the cutout shapes on the magnetic "face."

MOVEMENT

Flashlight Fun

Have your children point to their face parts as you ask questions such as these: "Where is your nose? Where is your mouth?" Then hang a picture of a face on a wall. Let your children take turns shining a small flashlight on the parts of the face in the picture as you name them.

RHYME

I'll Touch My Hair

I'll touch my hair,
>   (Do actions as rhyme indicates.)
My lips, my eyes,
I'll sit up straight
And then I'll rise.

I'll touch my ears,
My nose, my chin,
And then I'll sit
Back down again.

Adapted Traditional

SONG

Eyes and Ears

Sung to: "Frere Jacques"

Eyes and ears, eyes and ears,
Mouth and nose, mouth and nose.
See me touch my eyes,
See me touch my ears,
Then my mouth, then my nose.

Adapted Traditional

LANGUAGE IDEA

Retell the story "Little Red Riding Hood." Let your children say the lines about what big eyes, ears, and teeth Grandma has.

SNACK IDEA

Cut bread slices into rounds and spread on peanut butter. Let your children make faces on the rounds with raisins and dried fruit bits.

Turkeys

Turkeys in the Barnyard

Place a piece of butcher paper on a low table or on the floor. Paint your children's fingers and palms brown and their thumbs red. Then have them press their hands on the butcher paper to make "turkey" prints. When the paint has dried, help the children add eyes, beaks, legs, and feet with felt-tip markers. Also add construction-paper barnyard shapes such as a barn and a fence. Hang the finished mural on a wall or a bulletin board.

MOVEMENT

Turkey Strut

Use small pieces of masking tape to make turkey footprints all over the floor. Play music and let your children pretend to be turkeys strutting around the room. Whenever you stop the music, have each "turkey" find a footprint to stand on. Continue the game as long as interest lasts.

RHYME

My Turkey

I have a turkey big and fat,
  (Bend out arms at sides.)
He struts around this way and that.
  (Strut.)
His daily corn he would not miss,
  (Pretend to eat corn.)
And when he talks, he sounds like this.
  (Make gobbling sound.)

Dee Hoffman and Judy Panko

LANGUAGE IDEA

Cut turkey shapes out of construction paper and attach them to craft sticks to make puppets. Let your children use the puppets when reciting turkey rhymes or telling turkey stories.

SNACK IDEA

Use a turkey cookie cutter to make turkey-shaped cookies or sandwiches.

SONGS

Hello, Mr. Turkey

Sung to: "If You're Happy and You Know It"

Hello, Mr. Turkey, how are you?
Hello, Mr. Turkey, how are you?
With a gobble, gobble, gobble,
And a wobble, wobble, wobble.
Hello, Mr. Turkey, how are you?

Barbara H. Jackson

Gobble, Gobble

Sung to: "Pop! Goes the Weasel"

A turkey is a funny bird,
His head goes wobble, wobble.
He knows just one funny word—
Gobble, gobble, gobble!

Lynn Beaird

Feathers

Painting With Feathers

Give each of your children a construction-paper turkey shape. Set out feathers and containers of paint. Let your children dip the feathers into the paint and brush it all over their turkey shapes. When they have finished, let them stick their feathers onto the wet paint on their shapes, if desired.

MOVEMENT

Feather Float

Have your children watch as you toss a feather up into the air and let it float to the ground. Then let your children pretend to be feathers. Play appropriate music and have them float slowly around and around as they gently sink to the floor.

RHYME

See the Feather

See the feather
Falling down,
Twirling round
To the ground,
Drifting softly
Without a sound.
  (Put finger to lips.)

Barbara Paxson

SONG

Found a Feather

Sung to: "Clementine"

Found a feather, found a feather,
Found a feather on the ground.
Oh, I am so very lucky
A feather to have found.

Picked it up, picked it up,
Picked it up just like that.
I picked up that pretty feather,
Then I put it in my hat.

Found a feather, found a feather,
Found a feather on the ground.
Oh, I am so very lucky
A feather to have found.

Jean Warren

LANGUAGE IDEA

Tell a story while adding colored felt feather shapes to a felt turkey on a flannelboard.

SNACK IDEA

Before setting the table for snacktime, let your children dust the table and chairs with a feather duster.

Grocery Shopping

Grocery Shopping

Set out a variety of empty food containers such as cereal boxes, soup cans, milk cartons, cracker boxes, and yogurt containers. Give your children paper or cloth bags to use for shopping. Let them put items into their bags and take them out again. Encourage the children to name the items that they shop for.

MOVEMENT

Shopping Cart

Set up an obstacle course made of large cardboard cartons. At the beginning of the course, place a child-size shopping cart. Let your children take turns pushing the shopping cart through the obstacle course, trying not to bump into the cartons.

RHYME

The Grocer

The grocer sells you
Milk and fish,
Or any food
That you could wish.
So when you're walking
Down the aisle,
Give your grocer
A great big smile!

Diane Thom

We've Been Shopping

Sung to: "Frere Jacques"

We've been shopping,
We've been shopping,
Now we're back,
Now we're back.
We have got some apples,
We have got some apples
In our sack,
In our sack.

We've been shopping,
We've been shopping,
Now we're back,
Now we're back.
We have got some juice,
We have got some juice
In our sack,
In our sack.

Repeat, each time letting your children substitute the names of different food items for *apples* and *juice*.

Jean Warren

LANGUAGE IDEA

Put food items into a grocery bag. As you take the items out of the bag, incorporate their names into a story.

SNACK IDEA

Let your children select and "buy" food items to eat for a snack.

Sharing

Sharing Box Fun

Use this activity (as well as the other activities in this unit) to help your children start learning about what it means to share and take turns. Make a "sharing box" that contains two or three toys for each child. Place the box on the floor and let each child choose a toy to play with. Set a kitchen timer to go off after several minutes. When the children hear the timer bell, have them put their toys back into the box and choose other ones. Then set the timer bell again. Continue until everyone has had a chance to play with the toys he or she wishes.

MOVEMENT

Sharing a Swing

Take your children outside to swing. Bring along a tape recorder and a tape of children's songs. At the beginning of a song, start pushing one child in the swing. At the end of the song, have the child get off. Then offer the swing to a child who has not yet had a turn. Continue in the same manner until everyone has had a chance to swing.

RHYME

Getting Along

We know how to get along
Every single day.
We take turns and share a lot
While we work and play.

Kathy McCullough

Share Your Toys

Sung to: "Row, Row, Row Your Boat"

Share, share, share your toys,
Share them with your friends.
It's so much fun to share your toys,
Sharing has no end.

Let's all share our toys,
Let's share them with our friends.
It's so much fun to share our toys,
Sharing has no end.

Rosemary Giordano

LANGUAGE IDEA

Make sure each of your children has an opportunity to share during the day. At circle time, tell how each child shared and give him or her a special sticker or other award.

SNACK IDEA

Give each of your children an equal number of orange segments or apple slices. Then let the children share with one another.

Puzzles

Carpet Square Puzzles

To make each set of puzzles, select two different-colored carpet squares such as a brown square and a green square. In the center of each square, cut out an identical triangle or other shape. To use the puzzles, let your children fit the green triangle into the hole in the brown carpet square and the brown triangle into the hole in the green carpet square. Make as many sets of Carpet Square Puzzles as desired.

MOVEMENT

Puzzle Pals

For each pair of children, cut a posterboard square into two simple puzzle pieces. (Make sure that the pieces of each square fit together differently.) Mix up the puzzle pieces and give one to each child. Let your children walk around the room, fitting their puzzle pieces together until they find their match-ups. When all the Puzzle Pals have been found, play music and let the children dance with their partners.

Hint: Take part in the game yourself if you have an uneven number of children.

RHYME

Puzzle Pieces

Four little pieces
Sitting next to me,
One starts my puzzle,
Then there are three.

Three little pieces
Lying by my shoe,
Another piece fits,
Now there are two.

Two little pieces,
This puzzle's fun!
I found another piece,
That leaves one.

One little piece
Left out in the sun,
I know it must go here,
Now my puzzle's done.

Put together a four-piece puzzle as you recite the rhyme.

Jean Warren

Picking Up Puzzle Pieces

Sung to: "Ten Little Indians"

Picking up puzzle pieces,
Putting them together,
Picking up puzzle pieces,
Putting them together,
Picking up puzzle pieces,
Putting them together.
Now our puzzle is done!

Jean Warren

I Love Puzzles

Sung to: "Three Blind Mice"

I love puzzles,
I love puzzles.
Look at me,
One—two—three.
I take a puzzle and dump it all out,
Then put back the pieces lying about.
When I am finished I love to shout,
"I love puzzles!"

Jean Warren

LANGUAGE IDEA

Cut a felt shape, such as a car, into several puzzle pieces. Tell a story about the car as you put the pieces back together again on a flannelboard.

SNACK IDEA

Cut a sandwich for each of your children into four pieces. Let the children put their "sandwich puzzles" together on plates before eating them.

Grandparents

Grandparent Mural

Cut pictures from magazines of older men and women who could be grandparents and of young children who could be their grandchildren. Choose pictures that show a variety of activities. Place a piece of butcher paper on a low table or on the floor. Let your children choose pictures of grandparents and grandchildren. Then help them glue the pictures on the butcher paper. Add desired details with felt-tip markers before hanging the mural on a wall at the children's eye level.

MOVEMENT

Let's Do It for Grandma

Have your children stand in an open area. Then sing the song that follows and have them do the actions. Repeat the song, substituting *Grandpa* for *Grandma.*

Sung to: "Did You Ever See a Lassie?"

Let's clap our hands for Grandma,
For Grandma, for Grandma,
Let's clap our hands for Grandma,
Let's clap them this way.
Clap this way and that way,
Clap this way and that way.
Let's clap our hands for Grandma,
Let's clap them this way.

Additional verses: Let's stomp our feet;
Let's wave our hands; Let's nod our heads.

Elizabeth McKinnon

RHYME

Grandpa's Glasses

These are Grandpa's glasses,
　　(Form circles around eyes with fingers.)
This is Grandpa's hat.
　　(Stand hands on top of head.)
This is how he folds his hands
　　(Fold hands.)
And puts them in his lap.
　　(Place hands in lap.)

Repeat, substituting *Grandma* for *Grandpa.*

Adapted Traditional

Grandma's Coming Soon to Visit

Sung to: "She'll Be Coming Round the Mountain"

Grandma's coming soon to visit,
Yes, she is,
Grandma's coming soon to visit,
Yes, she is.
Grandma's coming soon to visit,
Grandma's coming soon to visit,
Grandma's coming soon to visit,
Yes, she is.

She'll be driving a red truck
When she comes,
She'll be driving a red truck
When she comes.
She'll be driving a red truck,
She'll be driving a red truck,
She'll be driving a red truck
When she comes.

We will all be glad to see her
When she comes,
We will all be glad to see her
When she comes.
We will all be glad to see her,
We will all be glad to see her,
We will all be glad to see her
When she comes.

Repeat, substituting *Grandpa* for *Grandma* and words, such as *big camper*, *blue car*, or *motorcycle*, for *red truck*.

Jean Warren

Have your children use photographs of their grandparents to introduce their grandmas and grandpas to one another.

Invite grandparents to come in and share a snack with your children.

Babies

HANDS-ON DRAMATIC PLAY

Taking Care of Baby

Set out a baby doll and items such as doll clothes, baby bottles, baby blankets, an infant bathtub, and a crib. Let your children take turns showing how they can take care of a baby by diapering, dressing, feeding, and bathing the doll. At the end of each child's turn, encourage the child to rock the baby to sleep before placing the doll in the crib.

MOVEMENT

Like a Baby

Have your children lie down on a large rug on the floor, pretending to be babies. Then ask them to do things such as roll around like a baby, wave like a baby, cry like a baby, crawl like a baby, and sit up like a baby.

RHYME

Baby

Rock the baby in her bed,
　　(Fold and rock arms.)
Stroke her downy little head.
　　(Stroke own hair.)
Hold her pudgy little hand,
　　(Grasp hand of other person.)
And tiptoe away, if you can.
　　(Pretend to tiptoe from room.)

Repeat, substituting *his* for *her*.

Beverly Qualheim

See the Little Baby

Sung to: "I'm a Little Teapot"

See the little baby
Soft and sweet.
Here are his hands,
Here are his feet.
If you hug and squeeze him,
He will coo.
He loves to be
So close to you!

Repeat, substituting *her* for *his* and
she for *he*.

Beverly Qualheim

LANGUAGE IDEA

Ask parents to donate baby pictures. Let your children talk about what the babies in the photos are doing.

SNACK IDEA

Serve baby food such as applesauce or some other kind of mashed fruit.

Growing

Comparing Hand Prints

Make a print of an infant's hand. Photocopy the hand print for each of your children on a separate piece of paper. Let the children make prints of their own hands next to the infant hand print on their papers. Talk about how much larger their hands have grown since they were babies.

Extension: Let your children compare their hand prints with a print of your hand.

RHYME

I Am Growing

I'm growing here, I'm growing there,
(Point to head, then feet.)
I am growing everywhere.
(Point to different parts of body.)
I see someone who's growing too,
(Cup hand above eye.)
Who could it be? Yes, it's you!
(Point to other person.)

Adapted Traditional

MOVEMENT

Growing Tall

Have your children crouch down near the floor and make themselves small. Then have them start "growing" up from the floor, taller and taller, until at last they are standing on their tiptoes with arms raised high.

Growing Every Day

Sung to: "Twinkle, Twinkle, Little Star"

When I was a baby small,
I could only crawl, crawl, crawl.
   (Crawl.)
Now I'm growing up so big,
I can run and dance a jig.
   (Run, then dance.)
I am growing every day,
Getting bigger in every way.
   (Stand up tall.)

Gayle Bittinger

I Am in Between

Sung to: "The Mulberry Bush"

Grownups are tall
And babies are small,
Babies are small,
Babies are small.
Grownups are tall
And babies are small,
And I am in between.

Vicki Shannon

LANGUAGE IDEA

Use photos of yourself as a baby, a young child, a teenager, and an adult to tell a story about growing.

SNACK IDEA

Serve a nutritious snack that promotes growth such as plain yogurt mixed with fruit and topped with whole-grain cereal.

Baking

HANDS-ON DRAMATIC PLAY

Busy Bakers

Let your children help make a batch of playdough, using a favorite recipe (or use the recipe that follows). Set out the playdough along with baking utensils such as pans, spatulas, and pot holders. Also set out paper baking cups and bakery boxes, if desired. Let your children pretend to be bakers and make items, such as bread, cookies, and muffins, with the playdough.

Playdough Recipe

1 cup flour
½ cup salt
6 to 7 tablespoons water
1 tablespoon vegetable oil
Drops of food coloring (optional)

Mix together all of the ingredients. Store the playdough in the refrigerator in an airtight container.

MOVEMENT

Making Bread

Have your children stand in a circle around a big pretend bowl. Let them help pour in pretend flour, water, and yeast, stirring around and around to mix everything together. Then have them pretend to knead the bread, pat it into pans, and pop it into the oven.

RHYME

Pat-A-Cake

Pat-a-cake, pat-a-cake, baker's man,
Bake me a cake as fast as you can.
Roll it and pat it and mark it with *B*,
And put it in the oven for Baby and me.

Traditional

SONGS

I Like to Bake

Sung to: "Three Blind Mice"

I like to bake, I like to cook,
See me look in my book.
First I'll decide what I should make,
Maybe some cookies I will bake,
Or if it's your birthday,
I'll make you a cake.
I like to bake.

Jean Warren

I'm a Little Baker

Sung to: "I'm a Little Teapot"

I'm a little baker
Making things to eat.
I roll out the dough
And pat it oh, so neat.
When I am all finished,
I put it in to bake.
Then out of the oven
The bread I take.

Repeat, each time substituting a word,
such as *cookies, muffins,* or *rolls,* for
bread.

Deborah Zumbar

LANGUAGE IDEA

Cut out magazine pictures of
various baked goods. Include the
names of the baked goods in a
story as you place the pictures on
a paper plate.

SNACK IDEA

Let your children help bake quick
bread or muffins to eat for a
snack.

Food Scents

HANDS-ON LEARNING GAME

The Nose Knows

Collect several plastic margarine tubs and poke holes in the lids. Place a familiar food item that has a distinctive scent in each tub; for example, peanut butter, a lemon half, an onion wedge, and a cinnamon roll. Tape the lids to the tubs. Cut out or draw pictures of the food items and cover them with clear self-stick paper. Let your children take turns sniffing the tubs and trying to match them with the pictures of the food items they contain.

MOVEMENT

Walk and Sniff

Select scratch-and-sniff stickers that are scented like various foods. Attach the stickers around the room where your children can easily see and reach them. Let the children walk around and search for the stickers. Whenever they find one, have them scratch and sniff it, then tell in their own words what it smells like.

RHYME

Smells Like Dinner

Smells like dinner,
Ummm, good.
I can smell the turkey,
Ummm—smells good!

Repeat, substituting the word *breakfast* or *lunch* for *dinner* and other food names for *turkey*.

Jean Warren

SONG

Ummm, Good

Sung to: "Frere Jacques"

Toast for breakfast,
Toast for breakfast,
Ummm, good. Ummm, good.
I can smell it toasting,
I can smell it toasting.
Smells so good!
Smells so good!

Soup for lunch,
Soup for lunch,
Ummm, good. Ummm, good.
I can smell it cooking,
I can smell it cooking.
Smells so good!
Smells so good!

Pizza for dinner,
Pizza for dinner,
Ummm, good. Ummm, good.
I can smell it baking,
I can smell it baking.
Smells so good!
Smells so good!

Let your children suggest other foods to
sing about.

Elizabeth McKinnon

LANGUAGE IDEA

Talk about how foods smell when
you prepare or serve the day's
snack.

SNACK IDEA

Serve foods with distinctive aro-
mas such as cinnamon toast,
oranges, or peanut butter.

Families

HANDS-ON DRAMATIC PLAY

Dollhouse Fun

Decorate several cardboard cartons to make simple dollhouses. For dollhouse people, cut cardboard tubes into various lengths. Using felt-tip markers, draw faces and clothing on the tubes to make babies, boys and girls, adult men and women, and older men and women. Let your children choose dollhouse people to make up families. Ask them to explain who the members of their families are. Then let them play with their dollhouse families inside the dollhouses.

MOVEMENT

The Family in the Dell

Stand with your children in a circle. Then sing the song below and act out the movements described.

Sung to: "The Farmer in the Dell"

The family in the dell,
(*Join hands and circle round.*)
The family in the dell.
Heigh-ho the derry-oh,
The family in the dell.

Additional verses: The father claps his hands (*Have everyone clap hands.*); The mother stomps her feet (*Have everyone stomp feet.*); The brother nods his head (*Have everyone nod head.*); The sister taps her toes (*Have everyone tap toes.*); The grandpa wiggles his hips (*Have everyone wiggle hips.*); The grandma twirls around (*Have everyone twirl around.*); The family in the dell (*Join hands and circle round.*).

Adapted Traditional

RHYME

Some Families

Some families are big,
Some families are small.
Some families are short,
Some families are tall.

Some families live close,
Some live far away.
But they all love each other,
In their own special way.

Jean Warren

Oh, Come and Meet My Family

Sung to: "The Muffin Man"

Oh, come and meet my family,
My family, my family.
Oh, come and meet my family,
I just love them so.

Oh, come and meet my mother,
My mother, my mother.
Oh, come and meet my mother,
I just love her so.

Continue singing similar verses, letting your children name a different family member each time.

Jean Warren

LANGUAGE IDEA

Encourage your children to share stories about what they like to do with their families.

SNACK IDEA

Invite members of your children's families to drop in and share a snack. Let the children help with the preparation.

Dishes

Sorting Dishes

In a box, place plastic plates, cups, and bowls in two or three different colors. Place the box on a low table or on the floor. Let your children remove the dishes from the box and sort them first by kind and then by color.

MOVEMENT

Stacking and Washing Dishes

Give your children plastic plates, cups, and bowls along with a plastic dishpan. Have the children stack the dishes in piles. Then let them pretend to wash the dishes in the dishpan. If desired, give them a towel and have them pretend to dry the dishes also.

RHYME

Playing With Dishes

I like to play with dishes,
It's lots of fun to do.
I play with bowls,
And plates and cups—
You can do it, too!

Elizabeth McKinnon

This Is the Way We Set the Table

Sung to: "The Mulberry Bush"

This is the way we set the table,
Set the table, set the table.
This is the way we set the table,
When it's time for a snack.

This is where we put the plates,
Put the plates, put the plates.
This is where we put the plates,
When it's time for a snack.

Continue with similar verses, each time substituting a word, such as *bowls* or *cups*, for *plates*.

Elizabeth McKinnon

LANGUAGE IDEA

Recite the nursery rhyme "Hey, Diddle, Diddle (page 52).

SNACK IDEA

Let your children help set the table at snacktime.

Favorite Foods

My Favorites

Cut out magazine pictures of foods that your children like. Let the children sort through the pictures and each choose several of their favorites. Give each child a paper plate. Have the children brush glue on their plates and place their pictures on top of the glue.

MOVEMENT

Waiter on the Run

On one side of the room, place different food items such as an apple, an orange, a banana, a potato, and a carrot. (Make sure that there is one item for each child.) Have your children line up on the opposite side of the room. Recite the rhyme "Waiter, Waiter" (this page), filling in the blank with the name of one of the food items. Let the first child in line run across the room, pick up that item, and bring it back to you. Continue reciting the rhyme until everyone has had a turn.

RHYME

Waiter, Waiter

Waiter, waiter
On the run,
I love _____.
Bring me one.

Each time you recite the rhyme, let your children fill in the blank with the name of a favorite food.

Jean Warren

LANGUAGE IDEA

Let each of your children tell you how to make his or her favorite food. Write down the "recipes" for making a group book to share with parents.

SNACK IDEA

Set out a variety of food items on separate plates. Let each of your children choose a favorite item to serve to the group.

SONG

My Favorite Food

Sung to: "My Bonnie Lies Over the Ocean"

My favorite food is ice cream,
It's what I just love to eat.
Whenever my dad gives me ice cream,
I say, "Boy oh boy, what a treat!"
Ice cream, ice cream,
It's what I just love to eat, eat, eat.
Ice cream, ice cream,
I say, "Boy oh boy, what a treat!"

Sing the song for each of your children, substituting the name of his or her favorite food for *ice cream*.

Elizabeth McKinnon

Pies

Playdough Pies

Make playdough using a favorite recipe (or use the recipe on page 118). Instead of adding food coloring, mix in some powdered cinnamon. Set out items such as rolling pins, small pie pans, and hot pads. Let your children have fun making Playdough Pies.

MOVEMENT

Pie Toss

Using crayons or felt-tip markers, decorate paper plates to look like pies. Have your children stand in an open area. Then give them the paper-plate pies and let them see how far they can toss them.

RHYME

Baking a Pie

The kitchen is so warm and nice
   (Hug self.)
And smells of apple pie and spice.
   (Sniff.)
Five, four, three, two, one minute more—
   (Count on fingers.)
Mother opens the oven door.
   (Open pretend oven.)
And then she puts the pie on a rack.
   (Set out pretend pie.)
Ummm, when we eat it, our lips smack!
   (Smack lips.)

Repeat, substituting other pie names for *apple*.

Ellen Bedford

Favorite Pie Song

Sung to: "Skip to My Lou"

Ashley likes apple pie, my oh my,
Ashley likes apple pie, my oh my.
Ashley likes apple pie, my oh my,
Ashley likes apple pie, darlin'.

Jon likes pumpkin pie, my oh my,
Jon likes pumpkin pie, my oh my.
Jon likes pumpkin pie, my oh my,
Jon likes pumpkin pie, darlin'.

Ask your children to name their favorite kinds of pies. Then sing a verse of the song for each child.

Elizabeth McKinnon

LANGUAGE IDEA

Make a list of the kinds of pies your children have tasted. As you read back the list, have the children raise their hands when they hear the names of their favorites.

SNACK IDEA

Let your children help you make a pie to enjoy at snacktime. Or serve pieces of a purchased pie.

Photos

Camera Observations

Set out an old, nonworking camera. Let your children take turns using it to snap pretend pictures of their friends and surroundings. Encourage the children to tell what they see through the camera lens.

MOVEMENT

Picture Perfect

Hold up a pretend camera (or an old, nonworking one). Tell your children that you want to take their pictures. Explain that they will have to follow your directions to make sure the pictures will be perfect. Have each child hold a block or other prop. Then give directions such as these as you snap pretend photos: "Stand next to your block. Hold the block over your head. Sit on your block. Put the block under your arm."

Variation: Use an instant camera to take real photos of your children at play. Show the photos to the children as soon as they are developed.

RHYME

My Own Camera

If I had my own camera,
This is what I'd do.
I'd take some pictures—
Click, click, click!
And give a few to you.

Jean Warren

SONGS

Click, Click, Click

Sung to: "This Old Man"

Click, click, click, look and see,
I take pictures, one, two, three.
Now, just say "Cheese"
And stand real straight.
A picture of you
I'm going to take.

Elizabeth McKinnon

I Love to Take Pictures

*Sung to: "My Bonnie Lies Over
the Ocean"*

Oh, I just love to take pictures,
My camera is ready, you see.
Oh, I just love to take pictures,
Please hold still a minute for me.
Click, click, click, click,
Take one, take two, take three.
Click, click, click, click,
Now you can take one of me!

Jean Warren

LANGUAGE IDEA

Ask parents to send in family
photos. Let your children share
their photos with the group
before using them to make a
book for your reading corner.

SNACK IDEA

Use photos of your children as
place cards for the snack table.

CHAPTER INDEX

PIGGYBACK® SONG SERIES
Repetition and rhyme
New songs to the tunes of child-hood favorites. No music to read.

Piggyback® Songs
A seasonal collection of more than 100 original songs on 64 pages.
WPH 0201

More Piggyback® Songs
More seasonal songs—180 in all—in this collection, which spans 96 pages.
WPH 0202

Piggyback® Songs to Sign
Four new signing phrases to use each month along with new Piggyback songs.
WPH 0209

Holiday Piggyback® Songs
More than 250 original songs for 15 holidays and other celebrations.
WPH 0206

Piggyback® Songs for School
Delightful songs to use throughout the school day. Favorites in this 96-page book include songs for getting acquainted, transitions, storytime, movement, and cleanup time.
WPH 0208

Animal Piggyback® Songs
More than 200 songs about farm, zoo, and sea animals.
WPH 0207

Piggyback® Songs for Infants and Toddlers
This special collection of more than 170 songs is just right for infants and toddlers. Also appropriate for children 3 to 5.
WPH 0203

1•2•3 SERIES
These books emphasize beginning hands-on activities—creative art, no-lose games, puppets, and more. Designed for children ages 3 to 6.

1•2•3 Art
Open-ended art activities emphasizing the creative process are included in this 160-page book. All 238 activities use inexpensive, readily available materials.
WPH 0401

1•2•3 Games
Each of the 70 no-lose games in this book are designed to foster creativity and decision making for a variety of ages.
WPH 0402

1•2•3 Colors
160 pages of activities for "Color Days," including art, learning games, language, science, movement, music, and snacks.
WPH 0403

NEW! 1•2•3 Science
A collection of fun and wonder-filled activities that gets children excited about science and helps develop early science skills such as predicting and estimating.
WPH 0410

1•2•3 Rhymes, Songs & Stories
Capture the imaginations of young children with these open-ended rhymes, songs, and stories.
WPH 0408

1•2•3 Puppets
More than 50 simple puppets to make for working with young children, including Willie Worm, Dancing Spoon, and more.
WPH 0404

1•2•3 Math
This book has activities galore for experiencing number concepts such as sorting, measuring, time, and ages.
WPH 0409

1•2•3 Reading & Writing
Meaningful and nonthreatening activities help young children develop *pre-reading* and *pre-writing* skills.
WPH 0407

1001 SERIES
These books are the ultimate resources for anyone who works with young children.

NEW! 1001 Teaching Tips
Busy teachers on limited budgets need all the help they can get. By combining the best ideas submitted to the *Totline* newsletter, we are able to bring teachers 1001 shortcuts to success! Three major sections include curriculum tips, room tips, and special times tips.
WPH 1502

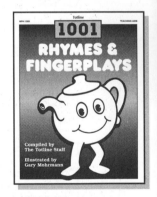

NEW! 1001 Rhymes & Fingerplays
This is the ultimate language resource for parents and teachers! Included are rhymes for every day and every occasion! Also included are poems about self, cooperation, and the environment.
WPH 1503

1001 Teaching Props
These 1001 ideas for using new and recyclable materials make it easy to plan projects, set up discovery centers, and make learning resources. Also includes a handy materials index!
WPH 1501

TOTLINE BOOKS

SNACK SERIES

A most delicious series of books that provides healthy opportunities for fun and learning.

Super Snacks
This revised edition includes nutritional information for CACFP programs and recipes for treats that contain no sugar, honey, or artificial sweeteners!
WPH 1601

NEW! Healthy Snacks
More than 100 recipes for healthy alternatives to junk-food snacks! Each recipe is low in fat, sugar, and sodium.
WPH 1602

NEW! Teaching Snacks
This book promotes the teaching of basic skills and concepts through cooking. Extend learning into snacktime!
WPH 1603

THEME-A-SAURUS® SERIES

These books are designed to supply you with handy, instant resources for those moments when you need to expand curiosity into meaningful learning experiences.

Theme-A-Saurus®
Grab instant action with more than 50 themes from Apple to Zebra, and more than 600 activity ideas.
WPH 1001

Theme-A-Saurus® II
New opportunities for hands-on learning with 60 more theme units that range from Ants to Zippers.
WPH 1002

Toddler Theme-A-Saurus®
Capture the attention of toddlers with 60 teaching themes that use safe and appropriate materials.
WPH 1003

Alphabet Theme-A-Saurus®
Giant letter recognition units are filled with hands-on activities that introduce young children to the ABCs.
WPH 1004

[Nursery Rhyme Theme-A-Saurus]

Nursery Rhyme Theme-A-Saurus®
Capture children's enthusiasm with nursery rhymes and related learning activities in this 160-page book.
WPH 1005

Storytime Theme-A-Saurus®
This book combines 12 storytime favorites with fun and meaningful hands-on activities and songs.
WPH 1006

CELEBRATION SERIES

Capture children's interest and enthusiasm with these teaching themes based on celebrations for special learning days!

Small World Celebrations
Multicultural
Teach children about other cultures with these multicultural hands-on activities that introduce popular holidays and festivals from around the world.
WPH 0701

Special Day Celebrations
Nontraditional units
Turn ordinary days into "special days" and get the most out of each learning opportunity. This book offers many suggestions for 50 fun mini-celebrations.
WPH 0702

Great Big Holiday Celebrations
Traditional units
This is the ultimate learning resource for celebrating all the major holidays. Included are ideas for hands-on learning activities for all kinds of celebrations.
WPH 0704

EXPLORING SERIES
Environments
Instill the spirit of exploration with these beginning science books that let you take activities as far as your children's interest will go.

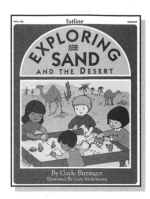

NEW! Exploring Sand
Set up a child-directed learning environment with this resource. Contains hands-on activity suggestions for learning with sand and about the desert environment and preserving it.
WPH 1801

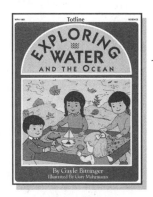

NEW! Exploring Water
This 96-page book is water fun at its best. Offers a full around-the-curriculum unit using water plus an introduction to the ocean environment with an emphasis on preservation.
WPH 1802

NEW! Exploring Wood
This guide for a child-directed learning environment includes activities for developing early carpentry skills and acquiring knowledge about forests.
WPH 1803

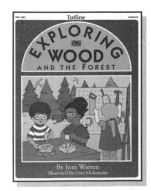